THE
SUCCESS
CAGE

THE SUCCESS CAGE

You've Built a Business That Owns You ... Now What?

P. BRUCE HUNTER

BPS
books
Toronto & New York
www.bpsbooks.com

Published in 2013 by
BPS Books
Toronto & New York
www.bpsbooks.com
A division of Bastian Publishing Services Ltd.

ISBN 978-1-927483-60-2 (paperback)
ISBN 978-1-927483-63-3 (hardcover)

Cataloguing-in-Publication Data available from Library
and Archives Canada.

Cover concept and illustration: Rob Ballantyne
Cover design and typesetting: Daniel Crack, Kinetics Design, www.kdbooks.ca
Text design and typesetting: Daniel Crack, Kinetics Design, www.kdbooks.ca

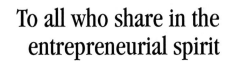

To all who share in the
entrepreneurial spirit

Contents

Introduction

This book was inspired by the many remarkable people I've been honored to coach and mentor. I believe there could be no more fitting way to begin the journey of this book than by relating two of their "aha" moments in their own words.

David's Story

I realized I had my priorities totally backward right after I said no to spending four hours of "us" time with my ten-year-old son in favor of my business.

My son was really excited that Major League Baseball's all-star game was to be held in our city, and he begged me take him. Without a great deal of reflection, I said, "No, I'm too busy with the business."

The look in his eyes hit me like a ton of bricks. I suddenly realized I had to take "me" out of the business. And that's exactly what I did. Guess what? The business didn't fall on its face when I stopped running everything. In fact, it got better. More importantly, I built a lot of memories with all my family. That wouldn't have happened if I had kept working *in* instead of *on* the business.

Mary's Story

My aha moment came when I learned to stop confusing the role of being an owner/investor with being an employee.

My partner and I had built our business on the back of what seemed to be several lifetimes of experience. We'd stuck together through more than our fair share of hard times during the early days, and things worked out for us. The company grew and we added some junior partners.

The story changed when the economy blew up. One year of struggle followed another. Finally, our accountant sat us down with some tough news: the business was in trouble. His advice was succinct and to the point.

"The business needs you to make decisions like owners, not employees," he said. "You've got to step out of the business and plan from that point of view."

It was the best advice we ever received. We moved ourselves out of the way and started providing direction vs. answers.

Entrepreneurs and business owners – people like David and Mary – are a special breed. They are builders and visionaries capable of creating new businesses in the face of incredible odds. Psychological studies identify five key traits that differentiate them from the rest of us:

- Risk tolerance
- Self-reliance
- Openness to new ideas
- Persistence
- Extroversion

They also share a secret pain. Once they've built their business, many of them suffer in the day-to-day management role required to run it. They feel trapped by the business and the weight of responsibility that comes with ownership. They either don't know how to let go or can't do so. They yearn for the day when they can jettison these responsibilities and get back to the joy of building again. They want to escape the cage of working on day-to-day business tasks as an employee and get back to what they do best – seeing around corners, or, as one of my clients likes to put it, "putting on the high beams for the business."

The Success Cage provides the tools for entrepreneurs and business owners to extricate themselves from this cage. To get back to their sweet spot and passion. And there's a wonderful side benefit. By reconstructing the business with them working outside the day-to-day tasks, they see its value skyrocket. This book provides candid insights, no-nonsense advice, powerful tools, and focused action for entrepreneurs and business owners who are seeking a path to rejuvenated passion for themselves and greater value for their businesses.

Throughout the book, I use business stories and examples to clarify information and bring it to life. It begins with a brief overview of organizational growth cycles highlighting the most basic construct, the S curve popularized by George Ainsworth Land. Following a discussion of the various stages of growth of a business and the characteristics and land mines of each of the stages, I invite you to take the first of several self-administered questionnaires. I created this questionnaire and administered it to over 600 CEOs and business owners before including it in the book. You'll be able to read about yourself and locate yourself in my staging system. The self-knowledge you gain will be an important underpinning of your future action.

The book then moves into a discussion of the differing characteristics of entrepreneurial and executive leadership. A short questionnaire will help you determine your orientation and will prepare you to consider the Big Five Psychological Factors of an Entrepreneur mentioned above. Then we turn to a chapter on the critical linkage between organizational growth stage and leadership style, one that contains a deeper analysis of the company. Another self-administered questionnaire will help you understand your company's strengths and opportunity areas by probing core operating strengths and needs. This questionnaire has also been used extensively in-market to help a wide range of companies set their go-forward action and planning priorities.

One of the key deficiencies of SME companies (small- to medium-sized enterprises) and their leadership is the discipline of planning. Simply put, they don't. I dedicate a full chapter to providing you with the world's best planning tool, the one page plan. There are many versions of a one page plan available in-market or over the Internet. I originally developed the version in this book to guide the integration of a $1 billion revenue company into a $2 billion company. The plan has now been employed by over a hundred companies of all shapes, sizes, and industries. It is offered as the structure from which the actions and priorities of the prior chapters can be executed.

The book's penultimate chapter is dedicated to helping you execute the plan. A plan, whether of one page or of telephone book size, is of no use if it isn't used. This chapter will help you put your plan, once written, at the center of your organization's future activity. The final chapter summarizes key learnings.

The Payoff

Why start a process to break out of the cage and move beyond the owner-doer model at all? After all, the majority of business owners don't. They choose to remain small and live happily ever after in the small niche they've created for themselves. They either wind their business down as they move to retirement age or transfer it at the appropriate time with little fanfare or return. And that's fine. There are a lot of happy business owners with small, successful businesses.

Destiny, however, awaits those who dare to move beyond the owner-doer model and out of the success cage. Because they extricate themselves from the direct day-to-day management of the business, they achieve an important goal and receive a handsome benefit.

The *goal* is freedom. These owners regain full freedom of choice. They are able to see beyond the immediate business to other opportunities. They are freed from the daily grind their life has become. They are freed from the feeling that they alone shoulder most of the responsibility for the success of the business. They regain lost energy and discover new passion. They rediscover relationships and purpose.

The *benefit* is usually wealth. Because the business is restructured to allow itself to move beyond the limitations of the owner-doer, it commands a much higher value – light years ahead of the value of a business managed by an owner-doer.

Talk about a win-win: personal freedom and a much higher return – an attractive outcome, to say the least.

I spoke with a very successful entrepreneur on the West Coast the other day and asked him to name his "tipping point." He said it was nearly his "breaking point." Here's what he wrote me later:

> At some point, your business will teach you that you can't do it all yourself.
>
> I was at my wit's end and ready to throw in the towel. The harder I worked the worse it got. It was bad. Until I realized that to grow, I had to let go. I needed a road map and someone to keep me focused. I restructured my role and my team, and the magic started to happen.
>
> Although it took some doing, I've moved away from the day-to-day in the business. I have a renewed trust in my team, and they now believe that I won't dive back into the business. Last year I took twelve weeks of holiday with my family, and I intend to take more this year. What's even better, I've just had a valuation done on the business and it has become much more valuable. What a win!

His aha moment came when he realized he couldn't do it himself. He couldn't work any harder. His relationships were failing. He was ostracizing his employees and family. When he finally realized he needed help, it came in the form of his team and a business coach – his personal business trainer – to keep him on the straight and narrow.

If you're reading this introduction, you've already taken the very important first step. You realize that something has to change. Change is never easy. *The Success Cage* builds from the collective experience of hundreds of companies and people just like you. It provides practical tools and the guidance you need to lay down your path to greater success. You'll learn how to expand trust to others and put your business in their hands. To drive accountability into your employee base.

There's a tremendous payoff in terms of personal and business freedom. You'll be breaking out of the cage you've created and set yourself on an exciting new path of passions and relationships you've neglected. In the end, you'll be happier and wealthier.

So, let's write your new story together.

Once upon a time, there was an entrepreneur who had built a successful business but found that, over time, the business had begun to run his life.

Every day, he went to work and found himself dealing with all kinds of people and process issues. Secretly, he started to resent the business and the control it had over his life.

One day, it struck him. He was working harder and harder to keep things together and spending less and less time doing the things he used to love to do.

Because of that, he decided something needed to change and he sought some outside help.

Because of *that*, he was able to put into action a plan to transform the way he ran the business.

Until, finally, he was able to break out of his success cage and go from working *in* the business to *on* his business. He had more time for the things he loved to do and wealth to do them.

And lived happily ever after.

1

Which Growth Stage Describes Your Business?

The sun was just rising as I sat in the restaurant waiting for my first appointment of the day. "I wonder what this one will be like," I thought as I sipped that wonderful coffee elixir. Just then, a well-put-together gentleman came through the door and looked around. My appointment had arrived.

"Over here, John," I said, pointing him to the chair across from me.

After niceties about the weather and various sports teams' play the night before, we got down to business.

John turned out to be a very interesting person with a terrific business and outlook. He was exactly the type who would make a good addition to my CEO group. He was a lifetime learner with solid values and a desire to share. At the time, my group, twelve men and women business owners, met once a month for a full day to share perspectives on one another's businesses and challenges. Outside these meetings, I also met with each person for a couple of hours each month to go a little deeper.

I outlined for John the group process and details about membership, indicating that he seemed to be a good fit. And that's when "it" came out.

"My business is different!" John said.

"Okay," I thought. "Here we go again."

John explained that his business had been around a long time and that he'd learned from this and that experience what worked well. Growing his business had been a long process of learning from experimentation and hard knocks. The industry in which his business participated was unique, he said, as was the experience that got him to where he was with the business. He was skeptical that anyone else could provide him with valued advice if they didn't have deep understanding of the industry.

More times than not, it starts this way.

I waited for John to finish his soliloquy, then said, "I think you'll find that **each business is uniquely the same**."

John was surprised by my flat-out contradiction of what he had just said.

I pressed on to support my point. "Each business owner, and, for that matter, each leader I have met with over the past ten years fervently believes their business is unique. Further, they all believe that unless someone has had deep experience with their industry, they're unlikely to be able to provide much value."

I told John that quite a different picture was painted by the evidence I had amassed from my own experience, the experience of at least 15,000 of the business owners in our organization, and the preponderance of the business literature.

"I agree that your business has its own DNA that makes it unique, but it shares characteristics and challenges that at least ninety-eight percent of the other businesses face at any point in their growth."

John arched his eyebrows at that statement.

Furthermore," I continued, "there's a pattern to growth. Each business follows a very predictable growth trajectory with distinct stages. Each stage has unique challenges, characteristics, and land mines. Understanding where you and your company stand, in terms of your growth stage, is critical to building a road map for growth."

I told John I was sorry if I sounded like I was lecturing him and asked if he wanted to hear more.

"Absolutely," he said. "Anything that helps me understand my business better and helps position me for further success, I'm all for it."

"Okay," I said. "Strap in."

Growth Fundamentals: The S Curve

I began with a précis of my own development in business and growing understanding of growth cycles. My fascination with the latter phenomenon began when I was VP of Strategy for a large multinational. The company, like many its size and age, had gone through a period of explosive growth through the post-WWII period. Unfortunately, that growth had slowed to a trickle. The company became more inward looking as it strived to meet the expectations of "the street."

Top-line growth for the company was more and more difficult to come by as markets became saturated and truly new products were harder to come by. To fuel the bottom line, the company focused increasingly on cost reduction, which, unfortunately, exacerbated the top-line growth challenge. As the company focused more and more energy on obtaining cost relief, its search for organic growth slowed. This created a downward spiral as cost reduction became more difficult to achieve once the low-hanging fruit had been picked.

As I stepped back, looking for perspective on the challenge facing us, I turned to a very simple concept I'd grown up with throughout my years in marketing: the idea of a product life cycle. If products had life cycles, why not companies? Cycles were all around us. Of civilizations, which were born, flourished, and died.

Of individuals (hatched, matched, and dispatched). Of organisms. I then turned to business literature to determine whether this phenomenon had been studied. Of course it had! By many! A number of prominent academics had developed conceptual frameworks to describe the movement of a business from inception to decline, rebirth, or death.

The simplest framework was built on the sigmoid curve (more commonly known as the S curve). There is evidence that this framework was used in the mid-1800s by Pierre François Verhulst, in the context of population growth. It is broadly applied to a number of fields of study, including artificial neural networks, biology, demography, economics, chemistry, probability, and statistics. It also forms the basis of George Ainsworth Land's seminal work on the growth of organizations and the challenge of change, *Grow or Die: The Unifying Principle of Transformation*.

Land postulated that the pattern of change that is found throughout nature is also reflected in organizations, with sustained growth being represented by a series of interconnected S curves.

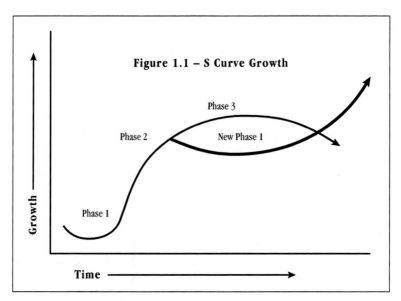

Figure 1.1 – S Curve Growth

Each such curve is divided into three phases.

Phase 1 is the birth phase, in which an organism or organization tries to establish a connection to its environment. If a connection is established (food, shelter, or a customer, in the case of a company), the organization survives. If not, it dies. This is the period of highest experimentation and, unfortunately, mortality.

Phase 2 is the phase of exponential growth. Because the organization has survived, establishing a connection to its environment, it can now focus on the task of replicating the successful system. The organization builds and becomes efficient in its go-to-market activity. It is able to grow rapidly because it doesn't have to expend resources searching for alternate paths of survival. It is focused and efficient.

Phase 3 is characterized by slower growth and ultimately decline and possible death. As the organism depletes resources (food, products, lines of service), growth slows. Unless a new resource is found, the organization stagnates, declines, and dies.

An Island of Growth

Thomas Robert Malthus (1766–1834), a British demographer and economist, used a simple illustration to explain the workings of the S curve. It goes like this: Imagine an island with a good supply of vegetation, no predators, and a hospitable climate. Now, introduce a pair of breeding rabbits and watch what happens.

Once on the island, the rabbits begin to consume its resources (the vegetation). In S-curve parlance, this is **Phase 1**. The rabbits have made a connection to the environment and are able to survive. Once their survival is assured, the rabbits do what they are known to do quite well. They replicate quickly, consuming the resources of the island as their population begins to grow. This is **Phase 2** of the S curve, the period of fastest growth. Resources are plenty, allowing the rabbits to focus on eating and making more rabbits.

Phase 3 is reached at exactly the point at which the remaining resources are equal to those that have been consumed. From here on, resources are depleted, and, unless a new resource is found, the rabbit population stagnates and eventually dies off.

The island analogy is helpful as a baseline for understanding a vast literature that describes the organizational life cycle. Although many thought leaders have built their own versions (e.g., Greiner's Life Stages and the Adizes Corporate Lifecycle), all use, as their base, a cycle of growth replicating the cycle found in nature. Some, like the above-mentioned Land, use as few as three phases; others, like Adizes, have ten or more. All follow a similar path. Birth to death. It's no more complicated than that.

It's also easy to build an understanding of an organization's requirement for sustained growth. As in our island-of-rabbits analogy, an organization must find a new resource to sustain its growth or face death. Timing is also important. The optimal time to conduct a search for a new resource is exactly when the organization is experiencing its greatest growth (which, unfortunately, is also when the organization is least likely to feel the need). From an organizational standpoint, this is when you have the resources to test and experiment. You have the time to see which of the seeds planted will successfully produce new resources. You can also afford to take a few wrong turns. Mistakes will not have a major impact on the organization's overall health.

Unfortunately, most organizations search for new resources too late, under the pressure of stagnation or, worse, impending doom. The pressure and importance of getting it right and finding that new resource increase as growth declines. CEOs and leaders have shorter and shorter runways from which to operate. The probability of success declines as the organization heads toward the brink. At this point, the business blows up, is reconstructed, or dies.

Land's framework helped me because it aptly described the situation my colleagues and I were facing at that large multinational I mentioned earlier. It also helped us identify the company's earlier pattern of growth. Since that time, I've worked with hundreds of companies of varying sizes and complexity and at varying stages of development. The S curve always proves to be a robust, simple, and accurate model of organizational growth.

The Organizational Growth Stages

John was obviously deep in thought. I asked him what was on his mind.

"Oh, sorry," he said. "I was just reflecting on your analogy of the island of rabbits. I can see I really need to get on with figuring out my 'next thing.' Our business has been going gangbusters lately, but I've also sensed a slight slowdown. Everyone else just feels it's part of the normal course of business, but I'm a little concerned. Somehow this seems more like a longer-term trend. Your analogy helps me to see it more clearly. We've got to get on this quickly."

I asked John if I could give him a quick overview of the system I developed to help others create a road map for their companies, and he was game. I mentioned that, after laying out the basic system, I could give him a questionnaire to help him figure out where his company was on the growth continuum, information that would help him build his own road map for continued growth.

"I'm all ears," John said, apologizing for the rabbit pun.

Navigating Smart Growth: An Overview

As I noted previously, a number of systems in the business literature describe the general stages of growth. The stages make intuitive sense and generally follow a development curve not unlike the stages of growth of an organism. Birth. Youth. Adolescence. Maturity. Old Age. Unlike an organism's growth cycle, however, the wonderful thing about a company is that, managed properly, it has the potential to last forever.

Examples of the longevity of well-run business may be found on www.bizaims.com, a website that documents the world's oldest companies, many of which have been built and run for over a thousand years. The oldest to date was Kongo Gumi, a construction company founded in 578, which was operated by representatives of its family through forty generations. It closed its doors in 2007 but still holds a substantial lead on the number-two company, Hoshi Ryokan, a hospitality business founded in Japan in 718.

Based on frameworks I have studied, my experience in business, and years of helping others with their businesses, I have created a growth cycle framework and have used it successfully with over 500 SMEs. It consists of five stages, each of which has unique characteristics, leadership needs, and land mines. Note that, in what follows and throughout the rest of this book, I deal at one and the same time with the organization and the leader. For example, I refer to both a company and its leader as at the Architect stage or the Engineer stage. There is no line of demarcation between the organization and the leader. People build businesses. It is the leader's development through the stages of growth that defines the speed at which the organization progresses.

The Architect: Validating the Idea

The company inception. The idea, which existed in the mind of the entrepreneur or small group, has received validation of its offering from at least one customer. The organization is created from the outside-in to fulfill the customer need.

The Engineer: Building the Go-to-Market Systems

In this second stage of development, the company's go-to-market mechanisms are fine-tuned. The business systems are built to support the sale usually of a single or limited offering.

The Conqueror: Expanding the Empire

The business has progressed beyond a single geography or product line. This stage sees the complexity of the business increase with new skills and specialization beginning to be added from the outside.

The Conductor: Building the Centralized Processes and Systems

Now a complex business encompassing many geographies and business lines, the organization transforms, requiring more process and discipline to manage a diverse and far-flung enterprise. Experienced managers and more disciplined processes are required to keep the ship pointed in the right direction.

The Renovator: Creative Destruction

Once a vibrant and exciting business, the business has grown increasingly inward looking. Growth has slowed to a trickle, often buoyed by financial engineering and cost reduction. It may have grown its own toxic ecosystem, focusing on itself rather than its customers. This is the end of the road. It must be renovated or die.

▲ ▲ ▲

I developed the following questionnaire to help business owners and leaders determine the stage their company is in. I urge you to answer this questionnaire yourself with your leadership team. (It works best when you get a cross-section of opinion.) Once you've done so, you'll be on your way to creating a targeted path forward for you and your business.

The Charge

Imagine you have just been hired to review the way your company conducts its business. For each item below, circle the number that you, in your role as advisor, believe most accurately reflects the situation in the business as it stands today.

1. Priorities and Resource Allocation

1	2	3	4	5
We do not have regular meetings to review priorities.			We meet regularly to set and review priorities.	

2. Liquidity

1	2	3	4	5
We never seem to have enough cash.			Cash isn't a problem for us.	

3. Planning

1	2	3	4	5
We have no written business plan.			We have a comprehensive written business plan.	

4. Management Structure

1	2	3	4	5
Our employees wear many hats.			Employee roles and responsibilities are well defined.	

5. Planning Horizon

1	2	3	4	5
Our focus is day-to-day.			We have a long-term focus.	

6. Business Processes

1	2	3	4	5
We figure it out as we go.			Our business processes are well defined.	

7. Employee Development

1	2	3	4	5
We have no formalized development programs.			Employee development is well established.	

8. Technology

1	2	3	4	5
We don't have a lot of tech infrastructure.			Our tech infrastructure is strong.	

9. Metrics and Feedback Mechanisms

1	2	3	4	5
Intuition plays the key role in guiding the business.			Metrics are key to guiding the business.	

10. Decision-making

1	2	3	4	5
Our CEO alone makes all the key decisions.			Most decisions are collaborative.	

11. Strategic Leadership

1	2	3	4	5
Our leaders are very involved in day-to-day operations.			Our leaders work *on* the business rather than *in* it.	

12. Organizational Climate

1	2	3	4	5
Things seem to change very frequently.			Change happens slowly.	

13. Organizational Purpose

1	2	3	4	5
The company's direction is crystal clear.			Our path forward is uncertain.	

14. Customer Focus

1	2	3	4	5
The customer is at the center of everything we do.			We are increasingly inward-focused.	

15. Business Growth

1	2	3	4	5
We are having trouble keeping up with our growth.			Lack of growth is a primary concern.	

16. Competitor Knowledge

1	2	3	4	5
Our competitor knowledge is low.			We have intimate knowledge of our key competitors.	

17. Focus

1	2	3	4	5
We respond to almost every fire.			We have a process to determine, and allocate resources to, our key priorities.	

18. Organizational Flexibility

1	2	3	4	5
We are nimble.			We bog down when dealing with new issues or opportunities.	

19. Risk Management

1	2	3	4	5
We embrace risk.			We are risk averse.	

20. Managing Employees

1	2	3	4	5
Our people policies are ad hoc.			We have strong human resource systems.	

21. Specialized Resources and Expertise

1	2	3	4	5
We have little specialized expertise in-house.			We have an abundance of specialized expertise in-house.	

22. Demand Forecasting				
1	2	3	4	5
Our forecasting is day-to-day.			We have strong and reliable forecasting systems.	

23. Succession Planning				
1	2	3	4	5
We have no succession plan.			We have a regularly reviewed succession plan.	

24. Employee Composition				
1	2	3	4	5
Most of our employees started with the company.			Our employee base is diverse.	

25. Leadership Alignment				
1	2	3	4	5
Our leadership is united.			Our leadership is divided.	

Add up the numbers you circled on each line.	**My score is _____ /125.**

Self-Assessment Scoring Key

Your score from the self-assessment questionnaire identifies your business's growth stage.

Architect	**25–44**
Engineer	**45–64**
Conqueror	**65–84**
Conductor	**85–104**
Renovator	**105–125**

Now that you've determined your business growth stage, turn to the next chapter to discover the characteristics and land mines peculiar to each.

2
The Growth Stages and Your Path Forward

The previous chapter highlighted the conceptual framework for understanding organizational growth cycles, which I have distilled into a five-stage model of Architect, Engineer, Conqueror, Conductor, and Renovator. By completing the questionnaire contained in that chapter and scoring yourself and your company, you've taken the first step toward building a path to your destination of choice. This chapter will give you deeper insight into all of the growth stages, but as you read on, pay particular attention to your current growth stage. Each stage is characterized by different needs, characteristics, and land mines. Understanding the stage you're in will help you move forward, whether your intent is to remain small and nimble or grow much larger.

The Architect: Validating the Idea

You are at the beginning of the quest to build a sustainable, enduring company. The business idea is being vetted and market-validated. You are energetic and driven. No mountain is too high to climb. You view the world as exciting and the opportunities as endless. You are a strong conceptual thinker, able to see the forest beyond the trees in front of your nose. You see clearly when others do not. The entrepreneurial spirit is reflected in the way you approach life and business. You have strong opinions, reflecting a confidence that few others possess. Because of this self-assurance, others may see you as stubborn and sometimes even egotistical.

Because your company is at the beginning of its journey, there is much to do. To this point, most of your time has been spent building and reshaping your business idea. You have spent endless days and countless meetings with potential customers pitching, getting business refusals, and re-pitching the business. It's likely that you are the sole employee or, at most, have banded with one or two others. You work long hours with little return. Despite that, your work is characterized by a spirit of adventure and camaraderie. If you do have partners, it's likely that they have skills that complement yours.

Your company mimics your personality and style. You run everything by the seat of your pants. The company has no formal processes, and everyone wears many hats. The business is structured around the people involved in it. Your market and product knowledge is largely intuitive and anecdotal. Opinions and processes and even products can turn on a dime – and often do – in response to customer whim. You do no planning. You are likely living from order to order.

At this stage of development, the future is yet to be written, so it is critical for you to remain open to ideas. Experimentation is at its peak. You are building an informal advisory group to help you in developing areas. You use informal networks and customer feedback to fine-tune business ideas and prospects. And you're perfecting your pitch through trial and error. Pricing is being tested, as are a number of other business processes: your approaches to distribution, production, and customer service are all in flux. Feedback on your offerings and go-to-market processes is extremely important to you.

As with any organism at the beginning of its existence, your business has the most tenuous hold on life at this early stage. Land mines and threats are everywhere. The most critical element, the lifeblood of your business, is CASH. If you have it, you survive. The greatest threat to any early-stage business is a lack of cash to run it.

Another land mine is perfectionism. Endless tinkering and stalling to make ideas perfect delays sales, which are critical both for the much-needed infusion of cash and the market feedback they can bring. You won't get it right the first time. Forget about it. Nike said it best: Just do it! The market will teach you how to adjust your products and services.

There are many other threats:

- Your own inexperience
- Venture capitalists who don't share the vision of the company and drive it too hard
- Mistakes that blow up the liquidity in the business
- Founders who lose patience
- Lack of focus – the "shiny object" syndrome many early businesses and entrepreneurs face
- Flawed ideas
- Poor market knowledge
- Overzealous discounting to get business
- Poor planning

Unfortunately, few businesses survive this formative stage.

The Engineer: Building the Go-to-Market Systems

You've survived the early days! Your company is becoming increasingly focused and understands its market position and offerings. As a leader, you feel confident and perhaps even arrogant now that you've been able to prove the sustainability of the company. You are passionate and driven. There's an evangelical zeal to your belief in your product or service. As a leader, you've built self-knowledge and have started to reach out to improve your external network. A formal advisory group is in the works, if not already established.

Many of the entrepreneurial characteristics that you exhibited in your early days are still in evidence, though they are tempered by learning and experience. You've had to move from dreamer to doer. The key focus for you and the company is building out the go-to-market systems and processes. Core processes of sales, distribution, manufacturing, and marketing are established.

The business still reflects your personality and style. You're bringing in new people as the company grows; it feels much like a family. The hours are still long but don't seem so bad because people feel that the work is contributing to a higher purpose. Communication is still informal, and people still wear many functional hats. Most gravitate to the tasks they enjoy most. There aren't many formal job specifications; many processes of the business are rudimentary.

From a customer standpoint, order patterns are becoming established. Unlike in the early days, you have moved beyond the point where a few customers represent the bulk of your business. The downside is that growth comes with a loss of customer intimacy. The upside is that you're becoming increasingly objective about the type of customer you'd like to have. You have established some forecasting and fulfillment systems. You're starting to create manufacturing standards and to focus on streamlining production.

Cash is still king. Although you've moved beyond living from check to check, your working capital needs are high and surprises can still happen. Because of that, you're developing more detailed forecasts and financial and cash flow plans. Expanding your market knowledge, customer profitability, lead generation, and sales systems are critical. Key functional competencies center on sales, manufacturing, and finance.

Survival is by no means simple at this stage. Many of the issues experienced by the business are created by the founders themselves. Entrepreneurial leaders often require all decisions to move through them, causing bottlenecks that can threaten further growth. Conflicts among founders can turn toxic. Arrogance, born of success, can cause over-confidence or missteps in planning. Planning on miracles, betting the farm on long-shot ideas, and the loss of key employees are but a few problems associated with the Engineer stage.

Growth itself is one of the key issues that you're facing. Problems exist at both ends of the growth spectrum. Grow too slowly and the business can implode. Grow too fast, and the business processes and cash requirements can't keep up. People are also a big concern. Because the company is relatively small, there is a very tight balance between affordability, numbers, and skill.

Employee turnover, loss of key experts, new hires poisoning the culture, environmental changes, system flaws, and premature processes are just some of the problems that can kill a business at this stage. And often do.

The Conqueror: Expanding the Empire

The business has now grown to a level of complexity that is likely to include geographic as well as product/service line expansion beyond the core. The founder is finding the management requirements of the business a growing challenge. The business has reached the great divide – between an entrepreneur/founder-managed business and a professionally managed firm. Many businesses fail at this stage, primarily because the founder remains too tightly in control and is not willing to change the way the business is run. Leadership needs to move from working *in* the business to working *on* the business.

To succeed, the business needs a very different operating model. It needs to move beyond the benevolent dictatorship of the founder as leader. The business leadership and the business itself need to accelerate the move to predictability. And that means creating a new bedrock for further growth. Systems, metrics, and new skills need to be brought into the organization. This is the most unsettling time in an organization's growth trajectory. Those who are unable or unwilling to make this change will often see their business fail or be sold.

For many business owners, this can be a troubling time. They struggle with a feeling that the business is moving away from them and their expertise. They understand the need to change but aren't sure how to accomplish it. Outside advisors are of particular value at this stage and can act as business sherpas to help both the founder and the business to transition. They bring a much-needed outside-in perspective and experience in steering a business in the right direction.

This is a vibrant time for the organization. It is growing and expanding quickly. The leader's focus is becoming more strategic. Leadership needs are changing. The need for growth to fund business activity is less urgent; the organization is beginning to turn inward to build the discipline and processes needed to handle its increasing complexity.

Decision-making is becoming increasingly fact-based and the culture is becoming more formalized. Facts trump passion and management by anecdote. The core focus that was evident earlier in the organization's life is widening to include other activities and lines of business. A bottom-line, rather than a top-line, orientation is emerging. Human resources systems are becoming refined, with functional expertise increasing and in-house communication systems being developed. More employees are also being brought on board from outside the organization, which has the effect of diluting the strong culture.

The company is breaking new ground in both its business and customer base. The pace of growth is forcing trade-offs in priorities. The need for planning and setting priorities is increasing. Feedback is harder to come by, both internally and externally. Customer intimacy is declining as the organization starts to create its own ecosystem. Innovation is becoming less intuitive and more structured.

Danger signs are starting to emerge as the organization hits the zenith of its growth rate. A number of potential land mines exist. Leadership turnover is a clear danger as founders turn for the first time to outsiders to run the company. Rifts between owner/founders and new professional managers can emerge for a number of reasons:

- The founder can't let go

- Professional managers are brought in who lack the delicate skill balance needed to bridge small and larger organizations

- Power struggles form up to fill a vacuum in leadership

- The core purpose of the organization wavers as new businesses and geographies are brought into play

- The company's focus is diverted from organic to financial growth.

- New competition emerges in the marketplace

The Conductor: Building the Central Processes and Systems

While the Engineer builds systems for going to market, the Conductor builds the company's central processes and systems to harness its proliferation of products and the various geographies it now serves. The complexity of the organization has now grown to a level that requires the special skill of a professional manager. The business has expanded well beyond its core geography and product line.

In many cases, the leadership of the organization has moved some distance from the business itself. Active involvement in business operations is transitioned to those with increasingly specialized skills. Decision-making has been or is being pushed down and out into the organization. Ownership is becoming increasingly distinct from management of the business. Formal leadership training is entrenched at many levels of the organization.

The organization is building and institutionalizing policies and procedures. Communication is formal, and systems are becoming more prevalent for carrying out tasks. Key functions have been, or are beginning to be, established. Human resources and management systems are being identified and expanded. Professional services and leadership, which heretofore were rented, are being brought into the company. Succession planning, training and development, and compensation and reward systems are well established. Customer management systems are emerging. Customer segmentation, channel differentiation, and competitive analysis and knowledge are increasing. Customer policies have been expanded.

Many new core processes are being developed and introduced. Formalized planning structures are being built. Business unit structures are emerging. Strategic planning and resource allocation methodologies are becoming more complex. Manufacturing processes are also being improved. Cost-reduction programs, such as lean manufacturing, are becoming entrenched. Crisis and risk-management programs are being developed. In the pursuit of growth, the company is seeking acquisitions.

The build-up of the more complex organization is also littered with land mines. Business challenges can come from a number of areas:

- Leadership may be inexperienced

- The attempt to centralize may fail or leaders may be unable to effect a change to a more complex and rigid culture

- As centralized control increases to provide strategic leadership for the units, a counterculture can take hold, with a commensurate loss of control

- In-fighting increases between the new "central committee" and those outside head office

- A we/they mentality can set in, developing either from the outside or the inside

- Increased complexity can also lead to loss of both focus and competitive inroads

- For employees, the new culture can mean loss of purpose or alignment

- "Old" employees are lost and, with them, corporate memory

- Culture and communication networks can fail

- Loss of customers represents a real risk as the organization turns inward

- Competition cuts into core product areas

- Markets can change

The Renovator: Creative Destruction

There comes a time in each organization's life when new leaders and a new direction are required to stave off decline and eventual death. Leaders at this stage are change agents. They have the unique ability and vision to set into place a new order that will cause the rebirth of the organization. Modern examples of this new leader are Lou Gerstner at IBM and Jeff Immelt at GE. Jim Collins's book *How the Mighty Fall* speaks of a number of organizations that, though they have achieved some measure of greatness, fail. Organizations entering this phase have some or all of these characteristics:

- The climate has become stale and toxic

- Company management and leadership have developed a sense of entitlement (think U.S. automakers). Indeed, the leadership of the company is like an aristocracy or a monarchy grown distant from its subjects

- Organic growth is a thing of the past. The inward focus that began in the Conductor phase has grown to the extent that the organization has created its own ecosystem

- Top-line growth is failing because the company has lost touch with its customer base and market

- Self-preservation is at the top of the leaders' agendas; the needs of the organization are playing second fiddle to those of a few individuals

- Leadership style turns away from an inclusive, more democratic approach toward an autocratic one

- Big initiatives designed to "fix" are introduced to the organization with increasing frequency, but often result in failure and leadership churn. The organization spirals in on itself

- Glory days are recounted with longing. The greatest focus is on reliving the past, not on building the future

- Employees "turtle"

- Communication is formal

- Excessive resource layering and delayering initiatives abound

- An underground rebellion begins to swell

- Cost imperatives become the focus, with declining marginal return

- More and more resources are needed to generate fewer and fewer cost savings. The company is in a death spiral

The Renovator could just as easily be called a Phoenix, creating growth from the ashes of the former company. Creative destruction is required to get the company back on its feet. The old needs to be rooted out and the cancer fully removed. New blood needs to be found. The rank and file need to become believers after sometimes years of enduring "the next new initiative." Innovation must be rekindled, most often starting with slow, small, steady gains rather than wholesale rejuvenation programs. Old processes and beliefs must be destroyed and replaced with hope. Customer connections must be rebuilt and new customers found.

Leaders must make the reconstruction visible and meaningful. They must start remaking and repurposing the company from the outside in. The conclusion of this stage is transformative. The company either lives or dies.

The Big Shift

The early stages of a company require nimble execution, fearlessness, deep creativity with scarce people and cash resources, and a boundless fount of optimism. Early days are frightening and at the same time exhilarating. Death stalks the corridors, and each day of survival is sometimes a cause for celebration. These stages are not for the faint of heart. It takes a very special individual to create and then breathe life into a new business. The entrepreneur/business owner possesses these unique qualities.

As the organization grows, it becomes more complex and unwieldy. Old systems and ad hoc processes become less able to keep the business on an even keel. Blow-ups and challenges become tougher to handle. The business shows strain as it tries to keep pace with its success. Gradually, and then suddenly, new business skills are needed. The business moves beyond the ability of the founder and requires a different skill base. That of the executive.

A critical distinction heaves into view here: the difference between entrepreneurs and executives. This is the subject of the next chapter, which is intended to help you see where you are on the Entrepreneur to Executive Continuum. This distinction is critical. It will help you understand yourself and how best to bring your specific skills to the benefit of your business.

3

Are You an Entrepreneur or Executive?

Building a path to where you want to take your company starts with understanding who you really are.

I was presenting to a group of business owners in Quebec recently, speaking about a major study that had summarized the fundamental and profound differences between the psychology of the entrepreneur and the executive. The broad stereotypes, which I'm sure you can describe, hold true. Entrepreneurs are "action Jacksons." They're full of energy, quick and responsive to changes in the marketplace, engaged 24/7 with their businesses, resilient and risk tolerant, and sometimes autocratic and self-oriented. In short, they're largely self-reliant and self-made. Executives may have strong entrepreneurial leanings, but, overall, they score much more strongly in team orientation, process, and planning.

Following the discussion, one of the business owners leaped to his feet and said, "My God! Now I understand why I've been having all this pain the last three years." He went on to explain his statement to the startled group. "Three years ago my company was bought by a much larger company. They have been trying to get me to look and act like those people you've described as executives. I DON'T EVEN LIKE PEOPLE LIKE THAT!"

Oil and water.

The skills needed to transform an idea into a company are very different from those needed to drive it forward to become a business of some size and complexity. I was asked one day by a thirty-five-year in-the-trenches coaching veteran whether I believed an entrepreneur could take his or her company across that Entrepreneurial Divide. After careful consideration, I replied that, to cross the divide, the entrepreneur will need to let go of the day-to-day and let somebody else handle it.

Michael Gerber, in his seminal business book *The E Myth: Why Most Small Businesses Don't Work and What to Do About It*, made a similar observation. He coined the phrase working *on* vs. working *in* the business. While the phrase trips easily off the tongue, actually getting there with a business is difficult for most entrepreneurs. The journey in reverse is as difficult for any executive who founds a business. Entrepreneurs and executives: they are two halves of a whole. The former excel in building. The latter excel in managing.

Transforming an organization to a larger entity requires the building of predictability into the organization through process and procedure. Entrepreneurs are excellent builders and visionaries. While they may manage well, their hearts belong elsewhere. To enable their businesses to grow, they have to let go. As one of my entrepreneur clients put it, "My primary role used to be looking around corners. I was great at that. That's where I should be focused, not managing the day to day."

Microsoft's Bill Gates, Apple's Steve Jobs, and Oracle's Larry Ellison are examples of founders who were able to achieve the transformation of their companies from start-up to monolith. How did they do it? Largely by being able to give up control of the process to those with a different skill base; by ceding control of the day-to-day in order to focus on where they excelled: providing the vision for growth.

So the starting point is for you to ask yourself the question, **Am I an entrepreneur or executive in orientation?** Deep down, you probably know the answer. Knowing where you lie on the psychological spectrum from Entrepreneur to Executive is an important underpinning for your successful business growth. The leadership characteristics required to successfully navigate from growth stage to growth stage differ markedly. The entrepreneurial leader is best suited for the early- to mid-growth company, the executive for the later-stage company. For an organization to reach its full potential, both types of leaders and skill sets are required at the right time and in the right measure. Understanding your orientation will help you identify where you best add value and, of course, where you don't.

▲ ▲ ▲

"I know now that I'm unemployable."

This line keeps coming up in one form or another from those I meet who are stronger in entrepreneurial orientation. It's usually followed by a story something like the following.

"I started with a larger company but didn't last too long. They and I knew there really wasn't a good fit. I couldn't stand the process that stood in the way of great ideas being executed. It's in my DNA to want to kill things. Most of the time I found myself sitting around attending meetings I felt weren't adding any value at all. I swear, half the time we didn't know what we were really meeting about. There would be a lot of talk with the primary action being scheduling another meeting. I had to get out and do my own thing."

On the flip side, I hear from a lot of executives who say their aspiration is to own their own business. While many have moved successfully from large organization to leadership of a small or mid-sized business, it comes with significant learning. They must learn to focus on executional and tactical excellence, an area they likely haven't experienced since their "early days." Here's a quick example of executives learning the hard way what it takes to build a business from scratch.

John, Mary, and Sue (names changed) left the employ of the company I was with to set up a consulting shop. Each would have been known in their former Fortune 500 environment as a HI-PO, or high-potential, employee. This is where the learning came in. The first thing they did was rent office space, buy computers, and put in phone systems. Given that they hadn't even talked to a customer much less knew where they were best positioned to service a customer, they soon had their first lesson in entrepreneurship: Cash matters! Having a paying customer also matters! To their credit, they survived the first year. They laugh when they tell the story now. It was no laughing matter when they were living through it.

▲ ▲ ▲

Following is a short test to help you locate yourself in orientation on the Entrepreneur to Executive Continuum. There are no right and wrong answers. After you complete the test, you will add up your responses to come to a score that indicates your psychological orientation toward entrepreneur or executive. The chapter concludes with an exploration of the Big Five Psychological Factors of Entrepreneurship.

Circle the number that corresponds most closely to how you see yourself.

I see myself as someone who:	Strongly Agree				Strongly Disagree
1. Is ingenious, creative	1	2	3	4	5
2. Perseveres until the task is complete	1	2	3	4	5
3. Tends to find fault with others	1	2	3	4	5
4. Is relaxed, handles stress well	1	2	3	4	5
5. Is full of energy	1	2	3	4	5
6. Has an assertive personality	1	2	3	4	5
7. Values artistic experiences	1	2	3	4	5
8. Is outgoing, social	1	2	3	4	5
9. Can be impatient with others	1	2	3	4	5
10. Has a strong, competitive nature	1	2	3	4	5
11. Is inventive	1	2	3	4	5
12. Is attracted to abstract ideas	1	2	3	4	5
13. Is relentless in pursuit of a goal	1	2	3	4	5
14. Generates a lot of enthusiasm from others	1	2	3	4	5
15. Has high confidence in own abilities	1	2	3	4	5
16. Doesn't shy away from unpleasant tasks	1	2	3	4	5
17. Is very sociable	1	2	3	4	5
18. Is direct	1	2	3	4	5
19. Is curious about many things	1	2	3	4	5

20. Enjoys a good debate	1	2	3	4	5

21. Is always active, on the go	1	2	3	4	5

22. Is efficient, organized	1	2	3	4	5

23. Is quick to decide	1	2	3	4	5

24. Is not usually worried about impression on others	1	2	3	4	5

25. Is industrious, hard working	1	2	3	4	5

Score (add up the numbers above)	_____

Scoring Range	Orientation
25–45	High Entrepreneur
46–65	Moderate Entrepreneur
66–85	Blended Executive/Entrepreneur
86–105	Moderate Executive
106–125	High Executive

Interpreting Your Score

This test has been developed from a body of research that has explored the psychology of the entrepreneur over the past fifty years. Given the brevity of the test, consider it directional in nature. It may also be useful for you to seek the perspective of others close to you. Have them complete the test with you in mind, and then compare your scores with theirs and discuss the results.

Like most psychological or personality tests, there are no right or wrong answers. We also have the ability to move our styles on the continuum to reflect the situation at hand. Over time and also in higher-stress situations, our natural tendency is to move toward our natural style. The purpose of this test is to help you understand where you feel you fit best. Entrepreneur or executive? This should help you map the best path forward for your company and your role in it.

The Big Five Psychological Factors of Entrepreneurship

In my work and in writing this book, I have reviewed hundreds of studies, articles, blogs, and reviews on the subject of entrepreneurship. The literature concludes that there is a closed set of five basic entrepreneurial traits, which are generally known as the Big Five Psychological Factors of Entrepreneurship. They are:

1. Risk tolerance
2. Self-reliance
3. Openness to new ideas
4. Persistence
5. Extroversion

Let's consider each.

Factor 1: Risk Tolerance

I spoke the other day to a colleague, who, like me, has spent a great deal of time with business owners and those who have built a series of businesses. I asked him what he believed was the single most important attribute that distinguished an entrepreneur from someone who was not. His answer was simple.

"To be an entrepreneur, you have to be comfortable with putting your house on the line," he said. "I've met a lot of people who were smart and resourceful and talked about being comfortable with risk. The true entrepreneur is somebody who's willing to bet it all. If they're not comfortable with that degree of risk, they're not really a true entrepreneur."

You may or may not agree with that statement. However, there is ample evidence across the vast majority of studies that one of the five key traits of an entrepreneur is a greater ability than the general population to tolerate risk.

What is the upside of having a strong tolerance for risk? The examples are all around us: iPhones, tourist space flight, personal computers. The list is endless. None of these would be part of the landscape today if not for entrepreneurial risk tolerance.

And the downside? It's just as obvious. Feeling impervious to risk can cloud judgment, to say nothing of causing the loss of money and assets when good goes to bad.

In my work I see up close and personal how people's risk-tolerance level is the dividing line between entrepreneurs and executives. I often have cause (unfortunately) to speak to those who are "in transition" from big corporations, the environment I toiled in for so many years myself. For the outgoing employee, termination of any sort is not easy to face. Many have been unceremoniously dumped into the market after long and successful careers. Most struggle to redefine themselves; many believe they can take their experience and parlay it into a start-up or the purchase of a small company.

The worst of these latter people are the cocktail party chest-thumpers. They believe (or act as though they believe) that running a smaller company or starting up a business isn't that difficult. Why, they've run businesses themselves, haven't they? Suffice it to say that few have the psychological makeup and risk tolerance to transition successfully to this type of enterprise. Most don't go beyond the chest-thumping for the benefit of the cocktail crowd. For those who do proceed, they are usually in for some tough lessons.

Factor 2: Self-reliance

This psychological trait cuts both ways. It attracts or repels depending on where you're sitting. The positive aspect, of course, is the power of self-belief. We're drawn to individuals who have the courage to lead and who demonstrate strength in that commitment. Steve Jobs, Bill Gates, and Richard Branson demonstrated a large amount of self-reliance when they built their businesses. The power of their conviction enabled them to withstand the naysaying of the early enterprise years and stay the course.

The negative aspect, self-orientation, is less attractive. I'm quite sure you've had occasion to meet "the smartest person in the room." As a mentor and "thought buddy," I find these people the most exasperating. Most have achieved a modicum of success, which they use to fuel their inner legend. I read one study that described self-orientation in business as being on a continuum from benevolent to belligerent, with entrepreneurs often populating the latter camp.

One of the more interesting findings I've discovered through my research, writing, and consulting is that there's not much new out there. It makes sense that the findings are, to some degree timeless. What differentiates an entrepreneur from an executive hasn't changed over the past fifty years. The differences have probably been similar for eons.

Supporting this particular trait of self-reliance, it has been consistently shown through the Survey of Interpersonal Values (SIV) that entrepreneurs demonstrate a higher need for independence and leadership while also scoring lower on the need for support and conformity.

Simply put, then, entrepreneurs have a stronger "me" orientation and a belief that they're in control of their own destiny. This is exactly the trait that makes it tough for them to relinquish control and why so many businesses are infected with acute founder syndrome. Think Research In Motion.

Factor 3: Openness to New Ideas

This is a tougher trait to characterize because it goes well beyond just being open to new ideas. It involves the unique ability to see patterns and solutions that others cannot see. Call it integrated thinking, design thought, or being innovative: the entrepreneur is much more adept than the general population at creating new linkages and systems.

I walked through a trade show recently with a friend who happens to be a serial entrepreneur. What occurred during that walk reinforced my belief in this factor as a major psychological trait of entrepreneurs. As we wandered the floor, she came to a stop many times to question the people manning the trade booths. So many questions! Why had they done this? Why not that? What was their experience with these? This happened time and time again throughout the day. I must admit I found it exhausting.

When our time at the show was over, I was spent. I looked around at my friend and what did I see but the very picture of happiness! Her energy had grown stronger during the day. As we sat down and shared our thoughts over a beer, she couldn't stop talking about the things she had discovered that she could apply to her business. She was bursting with new ideas she wanted to take back to her team. I marveled at her resourcefulness, energy, and enthusiasm.

Of course for every yin there's a yang. New ideas are the life-blood of every business, and new ideas can distract. I call them shiny objects, and entrepreneurs, in particular, are wont to chase them.

Here's a case in point. I was asked by one of my clients recently to interview his leadership team to see if I might help uncover opportunities to improve his business. It was quickly revealed that he was subjecting his organization to a stream of new thoughts. The organization was having trouble keeping up. He was the prototypical entrepreneur. He had started his own business from scratch and built it into a very successful consulting enterprise. As a consulting business, it was critical for him to be aware of leading-edge ideas in his field, which happened to be organizational development and business planning.

Unfortunately for his organization, his search for new ideas in thought leadership led him to want to share each of his discoveries with his team. And share them, he did … often. More than that, each new idea became an edict about how they were to conduct business and run the company.

It doesn't take a genius to guess the effect this had on the leadership team. "Turtling" doesn't begin to describe the skill they acquired. They met each request for change with feigned interest and practiced inactivity. They might do something if the leader showed sustained interest in an idea (three or more commands), but not with any passion: it was well known in the rank and file that a new direction would be coming soon.

In this particular case, all it took to get the organization back on track was to provide *that* learning to the business owner.

Factor 4: Persistence

To boldly go and stay the course. The upside of this factor is called persistence; the downside is called bullheadedness. In his book *Insanely Simple*, Ken Segall describes one of the underlying fundamentals that Steve Jobs drove at Apple. Segall observed Jobs from his vantage point as creative director at one of the ad agencies serving Apple during its renaissance. He writes that the philosophy of simplifying ideas and products permeated all of the company's discussions. He refers to Jobs's application of the philosophy as the Simple Stick. Jobs didn't call it this; others did.

Jobs applied the philosophy of questing for simplicity to everything he and Apple did. It could always be made simpler. How simple did ideas or products need to be? Unfortunately for many, the opportunity to simplify, in Jobs's mind, was infinite. Those who lacked the founder's obsession for simplicity got whacked with the Simple Stick and were sent away or unceremoniously fired by Jobs – a good example not of collaborative leadership but of entrepreneurial persistence.

You could probably relate a number of stories from your

experience or that of others demonstrating this trait among entrepreneurs. The adage "if at first you don't succeed, try, try again" describes entrepreneurs better than anyone else. The general population is less likely to get up off the mat as many times as the entrepreneur.

Here's another storied example of persistence in action, although in this case it is not about an entrepreneur but an explorer.

The British Trans-Arctic Expedition (1914–1916) is one of history's most famous "successful failures." Led by veteran explorer Sir Ernest Shackleton, the expedition's goal was to cross Antarctica on foot – eighteen hundred grueling miles across one of the most inhospitable landscapes on the planet, a frozen desert blasted by gale-force winds and temperatures colder in some places than the surface of Mars. But less than a day's sail from the continent, the expedition's ship was trapped by massive ice floes. Soon the *Endurance* was frozen tight in the impenetrable ice, where it remained for ten months.

Unable to free the *Endurance*, Shackleton and his men watched helplessly as the ice eventually ground it to pieces. They were marooned on sheets of floating Antarctic ice over a thousand miles from the nearest civilization with only three lifeboats and some supplies scavenged from the doomed ship.

The men had different notions of the best course of action. Some wanted to strike out in one direction, others in another; some were ready to simply give up. But Shackleton refused to allow the expedition to become paralyzed by dissent. He laid out a course of action and promised his men that if they all followed his lead, they would survive.

Under Shackleton's guidance, the men dragged the lifeboats across the shifting ice floes for another six months. Eventually the ice became so unstable that the expedition was forced to take to the boats, finally landing at Elephant Island, a dismal little rock covered by penguin guano and lashed by storms. Knowing his men were nearing the end of their rope, Shackleton then took the best boat and a small group of followers and set out for a whaling station on South Georgia Island.

When they landed, having survived an eight-hundred-mile journey across arguably the worst seas on earth and having been almost swamped by a hurricane, Shackleton discovered they were on the opposite side of the island from the whaler station. Currents made it impossible to try again, so Shackleton, despite having no climbing gear, resolved to take two men and cross the mountainous interior of the island.

Against seemingly insurmountable odds, Shackleton and his men did reach the station. With the help of men there, he returned to rescue his sailors trapped on Elephant Island. Amazingly, all of Shackleton's men survived in reasonably good shape.

Years later, when a researcher asked First Officer Lionel Greenstreet how the men survived such an ordeal, he answered in one word: "Shackleton."

Factor 5: Extroversion

You may or may not be familiar with one of the most widely employed psychological instruments, the Myers-Briggs Type Indicator. Based on Jungian constructs, this instrument divides individuals into sixteen different personality types based on combinations of traits identified as extroversion/introversion; sensing/intuition; thinking/feeling; and judging/perception. A study* showed that entrepreneurs scored consistently higher in three areas: extroversion (E) – an external orientation that promotes identification of opportunity; intuition (N) – an orientation toward innovation; and thinking (T) – an orientation toward flexibility and active response to change. In marked contrast, managers scored higher in the traits of introversion (I)

* J. H. Reynierse. Entrepreneurial Leadership and the MBTI. Panel presentation at the second biennial research conference on leadership of the Center for Applications of Psychological Type, Washington, D.C. (Cassette Recording No. 157-S16). St. Petersburg, FL: Convention Recordings (712-345-8288).

– an inward orientation; sensing (S) – an orientation toward detail and fact-based analysis; and judging (J) – an orientation toward a more structured approach and characterized by resistance to change.

It's important to distinguish between how we usually think of "extroversion" – as the trait of someone who is the life of the party – and how the term is used in this context. Entrepreneurs are not all outgoing, talkative sales folk (although many are). Extroversion means outward turning. A Wikipedia entry contrasts Extroverts vs. Introverts as those who:

- Are action oriented vs. thought oriented

- Seek breadth of knowledge and influence vs. depth of knowledge

- Prefer frequent interaction vs. substantial interaction

- Get energy from others

So What?

This chapter began with the words, "Building a path to where you want to take your company starts with understanding who you really are." If you didn't before, you should have a good feel by now for where you lie on the Entrepreneur to Executive Continuum. Those of you who have built your business from scratch most likely scored high on the entrepreneurial traits. Those of you who currently hold jobs in larger organizations yet scored high on entrepreneurial traits are probably unhappy with your lot in life or yearn for the freedom ownership would provide. The reverse is likely the case for those of you who scored most highly as executives.

Beyond giving you context and understanding, this chapter may have helped you see where you provide the most value to your organization. It may also help you identify your complement.

Every Kirk needs his Spock and vice versa. The entrepreneur (Kirk) needs an individual who has the skill and temperament to build process and structure (Spock). The executive (Spock) needs the spirit of action that is provided by the entrepreneur (Kirk).

Building Toward the Future

Now that you've reached a better understanding of where your company stands and a better understanding of your own traits as more of an entrepreneur or executive, you can undertake the task of building toward the future. Regardless of your company's growth stage, it's never too early to be thinking about building a business that is capable of operating distinct from its ownership. Each stage requires "right-sizing" the organization's systems, skills, and processes. Introduce these too early and you stifle growth; introduce them too late and the business is likely to stumble as it experiences heavier competitive challenges.

This is where the distinction I've mentioned several times – working *on* your business as opposed to working *in* it – really comes into focus. The benefits of transitioning to working *on* your business will be rewarding to you both personally and financially. Moving from *in* to *on* will allow you to get back to what you love to do: building and exploring. You'll rediscover your passion for your business and gain time to explore other interests and businesses. You'll feel relief as you unburden yourself of the part of the business you find less interesting and routine – running it. You'll become a new person to those around you and feel refreshed and energized.

Sound good? Of course it does, but as with all good things, it comes with a price. To grow, you'll need to learn to let go. If you're up for that, read on.

4
To Grow,
You Must Let Go

Earlier we looked at the various stages in an organization's growth. I don't need to tell you that the role of a leader in a privately held company is challenging. From inception, you are responsible for the success or failure of the company. The idea of the business likely came from you. You drove the early success as salesperson and evangelist. People were drawn to you and the business. Things got done because you, at the center of the maelstrom, drove the activity. The market and the success of the business – not HR or the board of directors – constituted your performance assessment.

And, in the early days, you had to fly blind. You had to make decisions for which you had no experience. Sure, you had a couple of people you could turn to for advice, but ultimately the big bets and decisions came down to one person. You made the hiring and firing decisions. People who needed direction learned pretty quickly that it was your input they should seek. Furthermore, the early-stage business likely also relied on your technical, sales, or operational skills.

With organizational growth, however, comes increasing complexity, and complexity requires different leadership skills. The imperative of company growth calls the leader to move from technical "doing" skills to softer leadership and management skills.

The movement from technical to strategic leadership is shown in the figure below. The figure depicts the degree to which each skill is required.

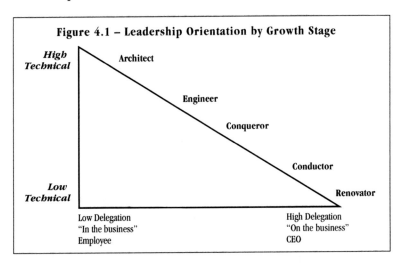

Figure 4.1 – Leadership Orientation by Growth Stage

In the early days, the leader is relied on for virtually all technical skills. Think, for example, of computer experts who move from their job in IT to form an IT consulting company. Initially, these individuals are relied on for their IT know-how. The business is built around them and their technical prowess as well as their customer relationships, which bring in the business. Similarly, designers who start a design business, marketers who start an ad agency, engineers who create a new product or system. However, as the business grows, the need for the technical expertise at the leadership level declines. The leader must, of necessity, shift attention to other areas. The build-up of company competencies. Operations. Accounting. People management. Legal. Marketing. The list goes on.

When this happens, entrepreneurs very quickly find themselves pushed out of the role they had originally envisioned for themselves. For example, instead of spending time consulting, they find themselves writing up performance reviews, organizing the next week of inventory, and doing a host of other such activities that, for the most part, are outside their areas of expertise and passion. They move from building and doing to managing, carrying a level of responsibility they hadn't envisioned and weren't prepared for. But they're smart, so they figure it out as they go.

I sat with a service company and their leadership team recently doing their (new) annual planning process. It was a great meeting – and a jaw-dropper for most of the team. During the meeting we began to talk openly about the need for the business owner to back out of day-to-day activities and move toward the more strategic role of working *on* the business. The jaw-dropper came when the CEO came clean about what he hated to do.

"I hate everything to do with running the business" was his statement to his team. "When I started this business, I was a designer. That was my passion. You don't need to wonder about why I like to get involved with the product we produce for our customers. It gives me the juice I used to have when I first started this business. It gets me pumped up again. In many ways, I'd like to get rid of all this other stuff I do and get back to designing."

This example underscores exactly why many owners and entrepreneurs choose to remain small as organizations or replace themselves as the leaders of the company. Very few find running the company as exhilarating as the "doing." The epiphany for many is that slowly, inexorably, they have moved into a role for which they have no passion. They find themselves wearing the mantle of the leader with no real sense of calling to that role.

The Big Question: To Grow or Not to Grow

There comes a point in every organization's growth when the entrepreneurial company either morphs into a larger, more professionally run organization or stalls. There is no right or wrong answer. For most, smaller is the preferred option. The industry refers to this type and size of business as a " lifestyle business." The owner is making enough money to support a comfortable lifestyle and has no desire to take on the task of growing larger, with all that entails. They keep the business to a size they can handle.

A Google search unearthed some interesting information. While these statistics are somewhat dated (2006/7), the UK Small Business Survey reports some interesting data that reflect broadly what we likely would find elsewhere around the globe. According to their study, "Business owners differ in their growth aspirations, perception of salience of resources and are often personally influenced by the anticipated consequences of growth. Growth aspirations change over time." The study concluded that a full two-thirds of companies can be categorized as "no growth." Fewer than 1 in 10 were seeking sustained growth.

So much for the illusion of grow or die!

The Global Entrepreneurship Monitor, again in 2007, outlined, by country, the percentage of small, early-stage companies aspiring to high growth (Bosma et al., 2007).* These numbers confirm the relatively low percentage of companies aspiring to high growth (defined as greater than 20% per year).

- UK, 11%
- U.S., 13%
- Canada, 15%
- France, 5%

This study confirms that, for most owners, operating on a small scale is a lifestyle choice. Many in the study identified growth as a desirable goal but perceived the risk associated with that growth to be too high, opting to stay small. Management capacity constraints and the lack of specific skills and experience for dealing with growth were the key contributors to the decision to "stay small."

---

* GEM reports may be found at <http://www.gemconsortium.org>.

Another conceptual model, developed by Robert Kiyosaki and called the Cashflow Quadrant, helps describe the movement from employee to investor. The quadrant and movement between quadrants is shown in the figure below.

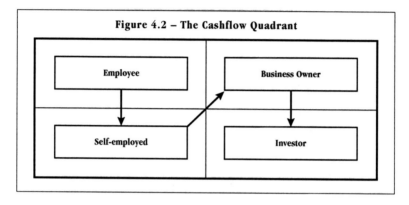

Figure 4.2 – The Cashflow Quadrant

Although Kiyosaki's model is intended to outline the type of returns available to each quadrant, it also helps us understand the nature of employees and investors in terms of the motivation, risk, and reward associated with each quadrant.

Employee

An employee is a person who earns money by holding a job working for someone else. This represents the vast majority of the working population. Employees are in the lowest risk but also lowest reward quadrant, unless of course they are able to move close to the leadership role in the company where they work.

Self-employed

This term refers to a person who earns money working for himself or herself. Canadian business statistics place the number of businesses in Canada earning over $30,000 per year through 2011 at roughly 2.4 million. Of this number, just over half do not have employees registered with the Canada Revenue Agency. These are the self-employed. Members of this very large group of people rely heavily on their technical prowess to attract customers. Many self-selected this type of employment, seeing an opportunity and the possibility of greater reward. This quadrant is highly populated by consultants and service providers.

Business Owner

A business owner is defined as a person with a payroll of at least one other than himself or herself. The number of businesses in Canada employing at least one person other than the owner is roughly 47%, or 1.1 million. Of this number, 99% have employees numbering fewer than 100. Medium-sized companies, with 100 to 499 employees, totaled 19,000, or .8%. And finally, those with 500 or more employees were 2,500 in number, or .1% of the total. Adding all of this up, it's clear how large this group of SME companies is in the landscape of business and how important it is to the economy.

From a development perspective, many of these owners report that they did not envision a business beyond themselves when they first decided to venture out on their own. As the business grew, it became apparent to them that they needed to bring on additional help: they became business owners by default. When asked whether they intended to build a business beyond themselves, an overwhelming majority answer no.

Investor

An investor is defined as a person who has moved beyond an ownership perspective and who may or may not have additional financial interests outside his or her company.

Business owners who move from working *in* the business to *on* the business take on an investor mentality. They view the business from the outside-in, becoming less personally involved in it. They see the business as a sum of working parts meant to deliver a return. They move from being servants of the business to having the business pay homage to them.

▲ ▲ ▲

So back to the key decision that you're eventually going to make. Ask yourself, "Do I want to take this business to the next level?" And ask yourself the corollary question, "Do I have the skills needed to do so, or if I don't, can I acquire them?" If the answer to these questions is yes, you have identified an imperative for a leadership transition from owner-manager to strategic leader and CEO.

The Role of a CEO

Imagine that you could be magically whisked back to the days when North America was being opened by the early explorers from the Old World. You are part of a team that has traveled across the sea from England, France, or Spain with no knowledge what this new land holds in store.

What role do you imagine yourself performing? Are you paddling the canoe, or are you at the stern of the boat making decisions about the direction and speed of the boat? People working in the organization contribute to the overall movement of the company, but they're not leading. They're doing. Business leaders, like those in the stern, are responsible to determine the direction of the boat even though they're moving into and through uncharted territory.

The CEO's responsibility, then, is to create the company's future by setting a clear direction (destination) and then to motivate and guide employees toward it. CEOs:

- Lead the development and communication of the **Vision** (Destination), **Goals**, and **Strategy** for the business

- Establish, track, and course-correct the key performance indicators

- Lead relationships with key company stakeholders (customers, suppliers, shareholders, government, community, and employees)

- Set the standard and model the behavior expected of employees

- Build and support the people plan

In a seminal article in the May 2009 issue of *Harvard Business Review*, "What Only the CEO Can Do," A.G. Lafley, the former (and at the time of writing, renamed) president of Procter & Gamble, lays out his prescription for the role of a CEO. He quotes the statement of Peter Drucker, the management guru, that "the CEO is the link between the *Inside* that is 'the organization' and the *Outside* of society, economy, technology, markets, and customers. Inside there are only costs. *Results* are only on the outside." Lafley further observes that "the CEO alone experiences the outside at an enterprise level and is responsible for understanding it, interpreting it, advocating for it, and presenting it so that the company can respond in a way that enables sustainable sales, profit and total shareholder return (TSR) growth."

One way to determine whether you're performing the role of a CEO or acting as an employee is the amount of time you dedicate to planning the future. Activities in this area include formal planning, reading, attending conferences, networking, financing, succession planning, people development, and meeting with key customers, government, and community. If the answer is that this type of activity takes up less than 25% of your time, you're most likely working as an employee vs. a CEO.

Dealing with this area of transition is my most challenging role as coach and mentor to business owners and entrepreneurs. The first tough patch I hit is self-knowledge. Owners who have grown their business from nothing to something, experiencing their share of adversity along the way, have earned some bragging rights. They have survived and learned some hard lessons that have become deeply engrained. Now someone comes along (that would be yours truly) and suggests that, to continue to progress, they need to drop a lot of what has made them successful and chart a very different course with a lighter hand on the day-to-day tiller. It makes for some very interesting discussions.

How can these leaders build self-knowledge? One of the best tools is belonging to a forum of peers. Many such organizations, global in structure, have sprung up over the past fifty or so years: YPO, Vistage (formerly TEC, The Executive Committee), EO (formerly YEO, Young Entrepreneurs Organization), and The Alternative Board, to name a few. As I've mentioned earlier, I am a former Chair of TEC, which provides a forum for CEOs and business owners from diverse backgrounds to come together in a confidential setting to share and learn about themselves and their organizations. One of the key values of peer group forums in general is the outside-in feedback members receive that is critical to their personal and organizational growth. It helps these leaders "know what they don't know."

This in itself can be an interesting exercise. Entrepreneurs, by their very nature, are not the type to flock together. It takes a special kind of person to self-evaluate and understand that he or she needs improvement in areas and then to do something about it. The great moment for most is coming to the realization that being a CEO doesn't mean having to know how to do everything and have all the answers. A CEO forum is a safe environment in which leaders can put aside their cloak of invulnerability and learn.

One of the key strengths of TEC (called Vistage outside Canada) is the way it mixes two types of outside-in resources. The first type is peer group and resource specialists, who are invited to speak to the groups, and the second is access to a mentor, or, as I called myself, a thought buddy. The two forums provide different benefits. The former gives members access to other entrepreneurs and the outside resource specialists in the form of speakers. The latter provides more "me" time for each entrepreneur.

The Peter Principle (rising to one's level of incompetence) is by far the biggest issue for those making the transformation from employee to CEO. It also dogs business owners and entrepreneurs who are trying to make the move from the Conqueror to Conductor stage of organizational growth. As companies grow in complexity, they very often outpace the ability of the business owner to run it successfully. Many (read most) owners have a difficult time letting go. However, as the organization grows, they must relinquish the tight control it was necessary for them to have at an earlier stage and replace it with a focus on delegation and hiring the right people. For those who make the transformation successfully, this is not an "event" but a process. Think back to figure 4.1 earlier in this chapter. As an organization develops, it needs to rely more on the CEO's softer leadership skills and less on the owner's technical skills. It doesn't happen overnight. Furthermore, as much damage can be inflicted by early abdication as by over control. Both can impair the organization.

The more common affliction is not under control but over control. I have many business acquaintances who have tried to cross over from a publicly owned company to help run a privately owned company, only to have been unceremoniously ousted by the business owner. It's a lousy place to be if you're the "hired gun" leader.

Here's a very common scenario. A business owner – let's call him Paul – has built his company from the ground up and is now approaching the Conductor phase of growth. Paul's comfort with running the company is waning as the business becomes more complex. He has received feedback from outside sources that he should step back from the business in favor of someone who can guide the company to the next level. Paul agrees and hires someone to do so.

Over time, however, Paul becomes increasingly agitated. The person he hired is making changes and, in his eyes, is not moving quickly enough, getting stuck with processes and procedures. Paul begins to seagull into situations (flying over, dumping, and leaving), thereby undermining the authority of the new leader right in front of employees.

Employees react more to Paul's actions than to his words. They see that the owner of the business hasn't really moved away from the business. They wait on his decisions rather than acting on those proposed or even ordered by the new leader. Paul remains deeply involved in the day-to-day running of the business.

As for the new leader, he is anxious to build the "right" kind of business but is experiencing "culture lock"; nothing much changes from when the owner ran the show. Eventually, the new leader is forced out or leaves and the organization stalls, or worse, implodes.

Managing the Transition to Working *on* the Business

One of the best tests of moving from a tactical to a strategic leadership role is the absence test. Here it is. If you can't leave your business for an extended period without contact (at least a month), you're still working as an employee. The transition from owner-operator to CEO involves consciously removing yourself from the day-to-day and building a management team to run the business. It's not easy! Up to this point you've been the front person. You've been involved in all the decisions. You like being the kingpin, even though the business is taking its toll on you and possibly some of your relationships.

The transformation is easy to describe but tough to do. You have to move from **"I do it all"** to **"they do it all"** as it relates to day-to-day activity. The carrot for you is freeing yourself to pursue your passion instead of being shackled to the business 24/7. You'll discover new interests and rekindle relationships. You'll feel like the weight of the earth has been lifted from your shoulders. It's worth it.

The following questionnaire will provide you with some guidance about your readiness to build and the appropriateness of building a new role working on your organization. Again, there are no right or wrong answers. You may be at a stage in the development of your organization that requires your presence and tight control. This is very likely the case if yours is an earlier-stage company. However, if you scored in the growth cycle survey as being at the Engineer, Conqueror, or Conductor stage, and you would like to grow your company further, you need to move toward this transition.

For each question below, circle the number that best represents you and your feelings today.

1 Disagree completely	2 Disagree somewhat	3 Neither agree nor disagree	4 Agree somewhat	5 Agree completely

1. The future for my business looks brighter than the past.	1	2	3	4	5
2. I'm still as passionate about the business as I was at the start.	1	2	3	4	5
3. I have a clear vision for where I'd like to take this company next.	1	2	3	4	5
4. I feel I still have the energy to guide this company to where I think it can go.	1	2	3	4	5
5. I'm still having fun.	1	2	3	4	5
6. The business challenges we're facing will be relatively easy to deal with.	1	2	3	4	5
7. I feel that I'm personally continuing to grow with my business.	1	2	3	4	5
8. I am my business and my business is me.	1	2	3	4	5
9. I don't know what I'd do if I didn't have my business to keep me busy.	1	2	3	4	5
10. I feel energized and engaged when I think about my business.	1	2	3	4	5
11. My family is very supportive of the time I spend with the business.	1	2	3	4	5
12. I am confident that we are still vibrant competitors in this business.	1	2	3	4	5

13. My employees remain strongly committed to my leadership.	1	2	3	4	5
14. If we needed a major cash infusion, I wouldn't hesitate to invest.	1	2	3	4	5
15. The business would suffer if I weren't here.	1	2	3	4	5
16. I'm always thinking of new ideas and ways to grow this business.	1	2	3	4	5
17. I feel I'm right up to date with new business tools and trends.	1	2	3	4	5
18. I have no urgent need to take money out of the business.	1	2	3	4	5
19. I am in good health and lead a healthy lifestyle.	1	2	3	4	5
20. I feel there are big things yet to accomplish with this business.	1	2	3	4	5
Score					

Scoring

Over 70: You are not ready to transition your role. You remain committed to working *in* the business for the short term. You believe strongly in the business, and the people around you do as well. You should be thinking about building the longer-term plan and the processes that will transform the leadership process for you and the business.

40-69: You have conflicting feelings about transforming your role with the business. On some days you feel energized and inspired; on others you'd like to just pack it in. These conflicts are most likely growing as time passes and are becoming more distracting. The urgency is increasing for you to commence serious thinking and planning for the leadership transformation.

Under 40: Time to get serious about your leadership transformation process. In fact, you need to make up for lost time. You need to put priority on building and executing the transformation plan for you and your business.

▲ ▲ ▲

Now that we've completed building a better understanding of where you and your company stand, we can undertake the task of building toward the future. Regardless of your company's growth stage, it's never too early for you to be thinking about building a business capable of operating distinct from its ownership. Each stage requires right-sizing the systems, skills, and processes. Introduce these too early and you stifle growth; introduce them too late and the business is likely to stumble as it experiences heavier competitive challenges. With that in mind, take a look at the story at the beginning of the next chapter. It may sound familiar.

5
The Turning Point

Jill sat down across from me at the restaurant. "Something's changed," I thought as I looked at her.

She started in. "Bruce, I'm totally stressed out. I went home the other day, sat down on the couch, and woke up there the next morning. Over the past few months I've never worked harder. I know you're always saying that I'm burning the candle at both ends, but this is different. I've always been able to keep my head above water. This time I'm not getting any relief."

Jill sighed and went on. "I simply can't work hard enough now to keep the place afloat while maintaining the connection to the business. I'm losing my grip on the business, my employees are revolting because I can't get to all of them to provide the kind of direction they want, and my family is becoming more than vocal about my presence ... or lack of it. I'm drowning!"

I'd been through various versions of this scene many times over the years and was sure I would continue to do so in years to come. Entrepreneurs and business owners come reluctantly to this epiphany – this "experience of sudden and striking revelation," as the dictionary defines the word. "Why does it always have to happen this way?" I wondered.

I thought again about Michael Gerber's words in his book *The E Myth*. He brilliantly describes the stage and situation Jill was facing. Here, in my words, is his description of the meltdown that is all too common in businesses like Jill's.

It's the beginning of a process of deterioration. The balls that you've thrown into the air begin to fall faster and with greater frequency than they ever did. You can't keep them all aloft simply by working harder and faster. Soon the thud of the landing balls becomes deafening.

You reflect on what you've done and your not so secret thoughts.

You never should have trusted anyone. You should have known better. No one is willing to work as hard as you work. No one has your judgment, ability, desire, or interest. If it's going to get done right, you're going to have to do it. So you do. But now, the more you do, the worse it gets. You can't stop yourself. You continue to do what got you here in the first place. You've got to go to work. You've got to catch the balls. You've got to keep busy.

Gerber points out the reality of this, that the business has grown past the owner, past the owner's ability to control it – to touch, feel, and see the work that needs to be done. The owner has reached a critical *turning point* for himself or herself and the business.

There are three possible outcomes.

1. A resizing of the business back to what the owner-founder can control. The resizing itself can be intentional, but, unfortunately, most often it is forced by a disruption of some kind.

2. A spiraling out of control of the business and its leadership, sinking all hands on deck.

3. A planned restructuring of the business and the owner's relationship with it. The business is rebuilt to allow it to prosper beyond the direct hands-on control of the owner-founder. It moves to become a smoothly functioning enterprise capable not only of sustaining itself but also of growing without the

constraints associated with the hands-on, one-leader leadership model. It frees the owner-founder to do what he or she does best – build, not manage.

Let's review again briefly the developmental steps that lead to the juncture reached by Jill and others like her. Entrepreneurs who create and begin to build their company are focused on surviving and feeding what seems to be an insatiable beast. The business is all-consuming! There's no master plan, nor should there be – at least not one that's written in stone. The business and those in it need the flexibility to react quickly to customer and market conditions in order to survive. The type of leadership required at this stage reflects the psyche of entrepreneurs: leadership that is persistent, daring, and non–risk averse. Elaborate planning and processes can be deadly to the survival of the enterprise at this stage of development and for many of its early years. MBAs need not apply unless they have the psyche of the true entrepreneur.

As the company grows, so does its complexity. We saw in earlier chapters that organizational growth and complexity progresses through several stages with remarkable consistency. Successful movement from one stage to the next requires a fine balancing act of introducing new systems, leadership, and people to the business on a just-in-time basis. Introduce these too early and you over-burden the company with process, cost, and loss of flexibility. Introduce them too late and growth stagnates and/ or opportunities are missed. The business is built into one that is capable of sustained growth by instilling increasing levels of discipline, process, and skills in the business and its leadership. An added benefit is that, generally speaking, the more the business can stand on its own two feet, the more value it commands.

Most companies go through their initial stages of growth without paying much attention to processes or procedures, much less codifying them. There's no time – or money, for that matter. In owner-operated businesses, which represent most of these earlier-stage companies, the owner is the business and vice versa. As in our example of Jill's business, the owner makes virtually all of the decisions and shoulders virtually all of the responsibility for the success or failure of the firm. That model works when the leader is able to touch most of the decisions and the people in the business. The vast majority of small- to mid-sized companies operate on the basis of a leader-doer business structure. These leaders work *in* the business.

Malcolm Gladwell used the term "tipping point" to describe the position and conditions necessary to take an idea or system to rapid, widespread growth. Likewise, my research across hundreds of companies of varying sizes, industries, and configurations confirms the existence of what I call a turning point for businesses aspiring to grow beyond that of a mid-sized firm. Jill's business had reached that point.

A successful transformation from the owner-doer model requires a fundamental change in organizational leadership, skill, style, structure, and processes. And that's precisely why few business owners and entrepreneurs grow in size from this turning point. Inertia on the part of the owner sets in. It is a powerful force that can be attributed to any one of a number of causal factors.

- The owner-founder has grown up in the business in a role that has become comfortable for people they know

- The prospect of substantial change is daunting and may entail high risk

- The rewards of moving toward a larger and more complex model may be financially attractive but not motivating. The owner may already have a very comfortable lifestyle

- Owners can't let go, suffocating the development progress

- They don't have a clue what they would do in a new role

- They don't want to let go ... for a myriad of reasons

But the reason that most often trumps all these is that they don't know how to do it. They don't know the path and don't have a business sherpa to guide them.

As these businesses grow, the business owners have slowly built themselves a cage. What started out as a dream of personal freedom, excitement, and accomplishment has gradually been replaced by an unanticipated level of responsibility, day-to-day headaches, and stress. Freedom from the cage is perpetually just over the horizon: "This year we'll get there!" But the freedom doesn't come. They continue to rely on themselves and the people and processes that got the business to its current level in the first place. And, unfortunately, the old adage holds true, that "what got them here won't get them there."

You may be asking, why begin a process to break out of the cage and move beyond the owner-doer model at all? The simple answer is that the majority of business owners don't. They choose to remain small and live happily ever after in the small niche they've created for themselves. Their businesses are either wound down as they move to retirement age or are transferred at the appropriate time with little fanfare or return.

However, as mentioned earlier, destiny awaits those who dare to move beyond the owner-doer model. By extricating themselves from the direct day-to-day management of the business, they achieve a goal of freedom and receive the benefit, usually, of greater wealth.

We started this chapter speaking of the entrepreneurial epiphany, the sudden realization entrepreneurs and business owners come to that they have created a cage for themselves and their business. A decision to break out of this cage is always accompanied by the stark awareness that something has to change.

It is said that overnight success is usually twenty-five years in the making. Similarly, this epiphany usually occurs after a process of significant thought about a problem. It may be triggered by a new and key piece of information but is most importantly preceded by a depth of prior knowledge and the result of significant study. Jill's "moment" came at the end of a long and circuitous route.

▲ ▲ ▲

We have now reached the turning point of this book. The goal of the forthcoming chapters is to help business leaders – and, in particular, entrepreneurs – build stronger, self-sustaining businesses.

We start in chapter 6 by discussing the core elements in creating stronger, more resilient businesses. As a follow-on, chapter 7 contains a "company mirror" in the form of a question-naire designed to reveal to you some areas for further development in order to improve the performance and value of your business. Chapter 8 outlines possibly the world's best business tool. It gives you a template for a one page business plan that will help you identify the core projects and activities you will undertake to transform your business.

Finally, in chapters 9 and 10, I provide some additional manage-ment tools and discussion centered on how critical execution and accountability are in the achievement of sustained success. In my experience, no plan, however simple and pragmatic it may be, succeeds unless it is used with discipline and rigor. Simply put, unless the plan is used and people are held accountable to deliver, nothing gets done.

So let's get going.

6
How to Build Your
Business into a Shiny Object

I sat the other day with John Warrillow, the author of *Built to Sell: Creating a Business That Can Thrive Without You.* In many ways, we're kindred spirits. We had a terrific conversation about his experience building and selling a service business as well as his focus as an author and speaker. Because I had spent a fair bit of time in mergers and acquisitions myself, our talk moved quickly to the key components that add value to a business. We were in violent agreement on one core premise: **There is no difference between building a great business and building a business with greater value.**

In my days of active M&A leadership, I had the opportunity to kick the tires of hundreds of companies, both private and public. I also had the opportunity to polish businesses to place on the market myself. Over time, I developed a list of business characteristics that increase the value of the business beyond just good financials and a track record. Most of these characteristics won't be found in a P&L or balance sheet. They are core characteristics that are built over time in steps and stages and that become part of the fabric of the company and its culture. Let's look at each of them here: core purpose, meaningful differentiation, strong people, solid infrastructure, and sustainable growth.

Call it your reason for being, your passion. Every successful business has a powerful reason for being. A core purpose.

In the movie *City Slickers*, Jack Palance spends no more than thirty seconds providing some penetrating advice to Billy Crystal about his core purpose (although he didn't call it that).

> Jack Palance: "Do you know what the secret of life is?"
>
> Billy Crystal: "No, what?"
>
> Jack with one finger raised: "This!"
>
> Billy: "Your finger?"
>
> Jack: "One thing. Just one thing. You stick to that and everything else don't mean shit."
>
> Billy: "That's great but what's the one thing?"
>
> Jack: "That's what you've got to figure out."

"What's Your One Thing?"

This is the simplest yet most difficult question in the world to answer – whether for yourself or your business. Why? Because it takes about a nanosecond, especially if you're under pressure, for you to start adding new things or directions, all the while thinking that you're adding value. It's not true, though, because the businesses with the greatest value are the ones with a core purpose underpinning all of their activity. These businesses are able to withstand market broadsides in turbulent times. Their sense of identity is like a sea anchor employed by old sailing ships. In rough weather, this special anchor was thrown over the stern of the boat. It provided the boat with improved stability and helped keep it on course. A strong core purpose works the same way for your business.

I sat with the owner of a service business recently. He was concerned about the position of his company over the past couple of years, feeling that it had lost its way.

"What's your rant?" I asked.

Not surprisingly, he looked at me as if I had two heads.

"What do you mean?" he asked.

"Most of the people who have built great, successful businesses started them because they either saw an opportunity or had a solution to a problem that they strongly felt needed to be solved. I call it their 'rant.' At the time they committed to building their business, it was a particular hot button. It's what they are, or were, passionate about. The business got built over the years because of that passion and focus. Not only that, it drew others to it."

I let that sink in for a bit, then said, "I'll bet you had something very particular that drove you to build your business."

"You're absolutely right about that," he said. "When we built our consumer research business, I was frustrated with the boiler-plate solutions that most companies in the market were providing to clients. Even the company I was working for had developed great processes but wasn't providing clients with real insight about the markets they were serving or their customers. They provided data and left the clients to try to figure it out."

He smiled ruefully at the memory. "I was almost embarrassed by our presentations. I started this company to right that wrong, and we've been very successful because of it. We attracted great people who felt the same about the problem and saw the same situation in the market."

Both of us left that meeting feeling refreshed and rejuvenated. He had rediscovered some of the passion that had lain dormant, and I had some new thoughts about how to help others going through a similar loss of purpose.

Another quick story about core purpose and the importance it plays in both attracting and motivating.

Along with several other senior leaders of a large multinational, I had scheduled a two-day conference to introduce employees to a new direction we were considering. The morning of the first day went well. We reviewed where we were coming from and where we were headed. We spoke of company achievements in terms of top line, bottom line, and margin performance. We also spoke of several key initiatives that had been undertaken and the performance of each. Finally, we spoke of the proposed direction of the company.

Following all this, we broke the employees into groups to discuss what had been presented. After about an hour of discussion, each table of employees selected a spokesperson to provide leaders with their feedback on our presentation.

We got an earful!

The net of the discussion was that we had missed the mark. We had tried to persuade rather than inspire and had spoken to what the new direction meant to the company vs. what it meant to each employee. I was reminded of a key lesson we'd forgotten during our exercise, that "people sign up with their heart, not their head." We should have remembered it's about inspiration. The majority of people want to make a difference. (Hold this thought; it will be developed further in chapter 8, which looks at how you can establish a Destination statement for your business.)

2. Meaningful Differentiation

Having a core purpose is an important starting point in building value. So is creating and sustaining a meaningful point of difference in the market. Just ask any marketing professional. There's no difference between building a strong brand and a strongly branded company. The greater the meaningful differentiation, the greater the value.

The literature abounds with the necessity of creating differentiation for your brand and business. For example, the books *Purple Cow* by Seth Godin, *Blue Ocean Strategy* by W. Chan Kim and Renée Mauborgne, and *Made to Stick* by Chip and Dan Heath reinforce the need to differentiate. I believe adding the word "meaningful" is an important nuance. It's important to be differentiated, but to create value you must be seen not only as different but as having utility. And that value is driven from the outside-in. It's not you, but your customers or clients, who define your value.

It is not difficult to grasp the concept of differentiation. It *is* difficult to pick and stick with your point of difference. One test I use to help companies with understanding the concept is to ask them to show me their website. Rarely do companies nail their point of difference there. In the case of service companies, very few limit themselves to one or even two services. Most provide a laundry list of services, their theory perhaps being that customers will pick and choose. The reality, however, is that the longer the list of services provided, the weaker the differentiation and perceived value. Tide used to stand for only one thing, delivering whiter whites. In my view, P&G has mucked it up recently by adding benefits and cross-branding, but that's a story for another day.

LEAP (name changed to protect the innocent) was a fairly typical mid-sized firm focused on helping business owners with their financial needs. Financial modeling, accounting, buying, and selling were among the many services offered. Business was OK but really hadn't moved up or down significantly over the past ten years. The owners were frustrated because it seemed that no matter what they did, the business didn't budge. They tried all kinds of ways to present themselves to the market. Radio and print advertising, free seminars – nothing seemed to move the dial. Until one day they decided to take a very different tack. **They narrowed their pitch.**

The owners of LEAP noted that, with a growing number of business owners reaching retirement age, more businesses were coming to market. Many businesses for sale and fewer buyers meant lower prices and less opportunity to sell. LEAP noted the strongly emerging trend of the management buyout, in which employees buy the company. This enables both management continuity and the positive option of a partial sale. This is where the brilliance of their next move came in.

Instead of continuing to pursue a multi-service approach, they chose to speak only to their expertise as management buyout specialists. They changed their marketing collateral, their web presence, and their pitch. They reinvented and marketed themselves as the world's pre-eminent specialists in this type of transaction. Their focus narrowed significantly. They further supported their position with case studies, testimonials, and value-added white papers on the subject.

Business boomed. Immediately. From the get-go, the repositioning of the firm paid huge dividends. Ironically, they not only got the business they had been seeking from management buyout activity, but they also picked up assignments across the service board. Customers assumed that their expertise in one aspect of finance meant they were expert at most financial services.

Here's another quick story to illustrate the power of differentiation. ABC Inc. was a transportation and logistics company. Unfortunately, everyone who owns a truck calls themselves a transportation and logistics company. Differentiation most often comes down to price, which, of course, is the last thing you want to compete on. I was visiting the company to speak to the president. We grabbed a coffee, and he began to bemoan his fate. I saw on his table a small leaflet that showed a truck and their service of handling hazardous materials.

I picked up the leaflet and asked him what it was about.

"Oh that," he replied. "That's a program we've been running for quite a while, actually with some nice success. It's higher-margin business than regular transport, and we've actually become more knowledgeable about how to deal with hazardous materials as a result."

"Eureka!" I said. "I think you've just found your point of difference in the market. I'm just a layperson, but it seems to me it takes a lot more skill and effort to transport hazardous waste. I suspect the average businessperson would assume the same thing. I bet becoming the company best able to deal with hazardous waste transportation would jump you to the top rung of the differentiation and quality ladder."

After a little more discussion, he took the leap of faith. Repositioned with a focus on transporting hazardous waste, the business took off. Customers rediscovered ABC. What's really nice about this story is that he eventually tripled the size of his business and more than tripled his bottom line.

Meaningful differentiation is a wonderful thing.

3. Strong People

"What's the single most important thing you've learned over the course of your career?"

I've asked individuals and audiences that question for years now. In one form or another the answer always comes back the same. People. It's people who create businesses. Great people create great businesses. Unfortunately, the reverse is also true. My next question is, "If this is true, why do so many of the business people I meet suffer mediocrity in their staff?"

In earlier chapters we looked at the growth of a firm from the Architect stage through the stages of Engineer, Conqueror, Conductor, and finally Renovator. The earlier-stage companies we described as being much like families. Employees are on-boarded not because of skill but because of familiarity and passion. The people who aren't a fit, for whatever reason, either self-select out of the company or are pushed out. Employees wear many hats and gravitate to the area and function of the business where they feel most competent. Of course that doesn't necessarily mean they *are* competent, much less best in class.

As complexity grows and the number of employees increases, the owner and/or management team find it increasingly difficult to achieve direct control. There is a burgeoning need for specialists with deeper knowledge than the founders possess. Here is another pivotal point in the company's development. To progress to the more complex, latter-stage company, the owner must hire beyond himself or herself in terms of skill. And that takes not only courage but also a strong ego – one that's strong enough to let go.

An experience I had with one of my clients awhile back illustrates the issue. Thankfully, this client had a great deal of trust in me and was willing to take a $40,000 chance that I was right. To this day (many years later), he still speaks of the situation and the fact that this single action probably doubled the value of his business.

Mark had a nice marketing and communication business that had bumped along for about twenty years. They had posted some nice gains in the early years, and the two partners, one sales and one creative, had built a great reputation among some high-flying clients.

Like many businesses, the company hit a wall in terms of size at about forty or fifty employees. One partner, for a number of reasons, exited the company after about fifteen years, leaving the other partner to run the business.

Mark and I started to work together after he had spent some time running the place on his own. After a couple of meetings, he confided in me that he was frustrated by the inability of the business to break through its historical revenue ceiling.

Mark's challenges were no different from those of a number of clients that I had worked closely with over the years. My challenge was to help him understand the value of a different employee and skill base.

Mark had worked for many years with a bookkeeper whom he trusted implicitly. She was dedicated, selfless, and hard working. The company's financial system had been built as the company grew and by now was held together with a tangled web of baling wire. (By the way, I see this a lot!) Julie held the keys to the system and how to get things done. That, however, was a problem. *Only Julie knew.* Sound familiar?

I'll reiterate at this point that Julie was a good person. She performed admirably when the company was smaller and needed to be nimble. To over-bureaucratize the business with financial controls, metrics, and systems could have been very costly earlier on in the company's life. Sizing skills to company development is an art. You've got to introduce the right skills and systems carefully, balancing the current with the future needs of the company. Too soon, and you blow the budget and screw up the business. Too late, and you don't capitalize on opportunity.

It was obvious to me now, however, that for Mark and his business to make progress, they needed another skill set. It was time for a person with the skills of a CFO. Therein lay the rub. I had to convince Mark that his loyal employee, who had been faithful and a strong contributor over the first ten years of the company's life, needed to be re-purposed and another person with different skill sets brought in. In convincing Mark, I had three major issues to deal with:

1. His loyalty to his employee, who had served him well.

2. His understanding of the new skills required to take his business forward and the value it would provide.

3. The cost. A CFO would add an incremental $40,000 above what he was already paying. Not an insignificant amount of money.

The task was to help Mark realize that his company now needed a CFO. Like many leaders of companies of his size, Mark was convinced the answer lay in someone who could be a rainmaker. To Mark, the problem was obvious. To break through, he needed more business; therefore a New Business Development person was the answer.

The answer for me was just as obvious. The business lacked

the financial bedrock on which to build a bigger business. It lacked controls, metrics that would promote smarter business and customer decisions, and the internal systems that would allow for greater accountability. We needed to shore up the base before we loaded a lot more business on top of it. How to break the impasse?

I guess I was lucky in two ways. First, for personal reasons, Julie resigned. While unfortunate, it was timely. Problem one dealt with. Second, as for issues number two and three, Mark made a move based on his trust in my outside-in perspective and made the move to bring in a CFO.

The change was immediate. Within a month, the new CFO had found more than enough money to pay for his salary. Within four months, he identified four times his salary in savings, not to mention making significant headway in building solid organizational processes. Mark was thrilled. A new day had dawned. In a year, he grew his business by 35% on the top line and doubled his bottom line. All because of a change in the skill set of one key employee.

I tip my hat to Mark. He made a very tough call without any assurances. Not long ago we were reflecting on this story, and I asked him what the biggest learning had been for him. I thought his answer was instructive.

"It was that **I didn't need to be the person to solve the problem.** When you build a business from the ground up, you have to rely on yourself for so long that your instinct is to continue to do so, even when you've probably hit your Peter Principle in terms of experience. I had to learn how to listen to others and trust the fact that they might have perspective I didn't. **I needed to learn how to work through others rather than through myself.**"

One of the more interesting exercises I do with clients takes no more than three minutes to complete, yet it ends with very significant discussion and action. Try it yourself.

Write down the names of your direct reports and/or partners. Within three minutes, assess each one as a 6 or a 9 out of 10. Now identify a plan to deal with the 6's and replace them with 9's because you can't afford to suffer the 6's in your business.

It's quick and often painful. I've even had a couple of occasions when a business owner wrote his own name and rated himself a 6.

This simple exercise will go a long way toward improving the value and transferability of your business. The stronger the management team and employee base, the more self-sustaining and attractive the business.

4. Solid Infrastructure

"Snips and snails and puppy dog tails."

If, as the old poem goes, "That's what little boys are made of," then the early- to mid-stage companies are held together by baling wire and bubble gum. Those systems and the infrastructure supporting them must eventually be replaced if the organization is to progress through the Engineer and Conqueror stage of our earlier discussion to that of the Conductor. In addition to the major changes required of the leadership of the company to progress beyond what I described earlier as the Entrepreneurial Divide, so, too, does the infrastructure and information base of the company. The stronger the infrastructure and information systems, the more valuable the company.

The move from earlier-stage company infrastructure is quite possibly one of the most difficult but transformative in the growth cycle of a company. It enables the move from a culture built on anecdotes to one based on fact and feedback. It represents the most disruptive period in the life of the company because it requires a major change in culture across every facet of the business. Here's a quick story to illustrate both the power of the change and the dislocation it can represent.

Ontario Hardware (a fictional company based on a real-life situation) was a business-to-business company supplying hardware parts to a very wide customer base in North America. It had a very large base of SKUs (stock keeping units) numbering in the tens of thousands. The company had grown from a small mom-and-pop shop over fifty years and did a magnificent job of servicing its customers from a number of warehouses that doubled as retail outlets. The sales and service infrastructure, as well as the Finance and IT systems, had grown with the company over time.

When asked to describe the system, an accountant friend of mine likened it to an extraterrestrial. As an outsider, it was so unrecognizable to him he was sure it came from some other place. Certainly not from Earth. Somehow the employees who grew up with it made it work, quirky and inefficient as it was.

There was a huge problem with the system, however. Not only was it holding the company back, it was threatening to be the root cause of the company's demise. Why? Because its major competitor had long ago invested in the type of infrastructure and systems that supplied it with real-time, accurate information about all of the facets of its organization. That company had invested in an ERP (Enterprise Resource Planning) system that merged the external and internal financial information and structured much of the company's resources around it. This move, although disruptive and expensive, had, in effect, created a new brain for the organization.

The change that occurred over the next two years at this competitor was like going from night to day. Sales soared, driven by smart systems that drove improvements in customer knowledge and service. The internal systems drove improvements in effectiveness and efficiency, dropping loads of cash to the bottom line. That cash became available for further improvements and investment. Feedback loops were created, analyzed, and acted on. Beyond the infrastructure, the growth and improvement in sophistication attracted the attention of people outside the organization. All of a sudden, it had the pick of the crop when it came to employees. And those employees who remained with the firm wanted to stay. Who doesn't want to work for a winner?

This situation involved massive change. Sure, the benefits ended up being worth the effort, but at the same time, it easily could have killed the company. Who's going to volunteer for that kind of a gamble and under what circumstances? Would you?

Back to Ontario Hardware. It had to make a choice. Would it die the death of a thousand cuts or face reality and start making the change it needed to survive. Here's the rub, however. The hurt the competition was putting on Ontario Hardware wasn't a cataclysm. It was a slow creep. Slowly, inexorably, Ontario was sinking into the quicksand. It's one thing to be forced to act to survive by imminent danger. It's another to realize you need to act when it seems that decisions and actions can always be made tomorrow. That's the situation that faces the great majority of the companies and the leaders I work with.

One blogger I read recently amused me with a description of a similar situation. He called it "perma five." What's that? It's the business owner's answer when asked, "When are you going to change your systems?" It doesn't matter whether the question was asked a few years ago or will be asked a few years hence. The answer will always be in five years. Because owners always believe something will somehow change miraculously and action will be taken. Only nothing really changes and nothing is done. Perma five.

I will tell you as a postscript to this story that the owner of Ontario Hardware did bite the bullet. He opted to go through the change and, yes, it was quite the challenge. It took inspired leadership, guts, and determination. It also transformed the company into a sleek, smooth-running enterprise.

Here's one last thought on infrastructure. If you're a business founder-entrepreneur, ask yourself honestly whether you're the person to undertake this type of systems or organizational transformation. There's a reason that chapter 3 above speaks to the psychological makeup of the entrepreneur. You, and the vast majority of other entrepreneurs, built your company from scratch and love to build, not manage. Unless you feel you have both the aptitude and passion for dealing with the administrative details of this type of change, you should place the duty on the shoulders of a good COO, GM, or CFO. A study I commissioned asked over 500 CEOs this question: "What, in retrospect, would you have done differently now that you look back over the growth of your company?" The answer was simple and direct: "I would have hired a great administrator much sooner."

5. Sustainable Growth

Earlier I mentioned George Ainsworth Land and his theory of how organizations transform and grow. I believe he hits the nail on the head with his title *Grow or Die*. A culture of learning and growth in a company is key to its ability to sustain its health, whether it is moving from growth stage to growth stage or not. Growth must occur just to sustain your position, much less advance.

The concept of sustainable growth, according to Wikipedia, was developed by Robert C. Higgins. It is a financial measurement that reveals the maximum growth a company can achieve within a specified financial strategy. Google "sustainable growth" and you'll be inundated with financial ratios and calculations.

My version of sustainable growth is less rigorous. Here is how I word it:

Sustainable growth is the rate that optimizes the right scale, depth, and allocation of resources within the company to allow it to succeed within its current growth stage while seeding the skills and infrastructure needed for the next.

Sustainable growth, therefore, is the outcome of the right balance of skills, products, and resources for each stage of a company's growth. The reality is that, over time, growth is not a uniform process. Growth is achieved through leaps and lurches. Periods of stagnation and breakthrough. The trick to achieving sustainable growth is to know where you are in your growth stage, understand the land mines you are likely to face, and put the right plans in place to guide your organization through the minefields to the next level.

Chapters 1 and 2 provided you with the wherewithal to determine your company growth stage and identify some of the characteristics and land mines. The next chapter provides you with an additional questionnaire that will help you lay out your road map forward.

Growth Challenges

There are three kinds of growth challenge, each of which can be experienced in every growth stage: not enough growth, too much growth, and the wrong kind of growth.

1. Not Enough Growth

When people think about a "growth" problem, they usually think about this category of growth issue first. For the early-stage company, it's finding enough growth to provide the resources to grow. Of course, at the very beginning it's about finding any growth. A purchase order. For the later-stage organization, it's about finding growth for survival.

Earlier we looked at the issues surrounding the late

Conductor-stage company that had become large enough to create its own ecosystem. As such an organization turns inward to satisfy the needs of the bureaucracy, it loses touch with its customer base and becomes less and less relevant. Just maintaining the customer connection becomes a monumental task. It's really no wonder that, as our economy moves into a more mature phase, more and more businesses are struggling with this type of growth issue. In many ways, the late Conductor-stage company needs a good shot of entrepreneurship to keep it afloat.

The issue, of course, is that the systems and bureaucracy of the larger company have grown so strong that most of the time they crush the life out of anything new. As proof, take a look at how many of a larger organization's acquisitions of smaller, growth-oriented companies succeed and contribute to its growth. Few. In fact, a recent study quoted by Dan and Chip Heath in their new book *Decisive* indicated that **83% of acquisitions fail to add shareholder value**. Most are sucked into the vortex of the larger beast. The growth that is so desperately needed is actually diminished as the organization sucks the life out of the new entity. A sad but very common state of affairs.

2. Too Much Growth

You can get too much of a good thing.

One of my dearest friends works for a large multinational retail organization. She told me a story that endeared her organization to me forever.

A little background. The search for new products to differentiate, refresh, and grow is always on the agenda for forward-looking retailers. Many times they get their best ideas not from the larger customers that call on them but from smaller Architect- or Engineer-stage companies. This is a particularly fragile period for companies in these growth stages as they neither have the infrastructure nor the resources to take on significant growth. Cash is almost non-existent. Certainly there isn't enough to support the working capital needed for very large orders.

The buyers at my friend's retail organization understood the issues facing a particular small company that had come courting them for business. They had a unique product that looked like a terrific thing for the retailer to introduce to the public. The issue was the potential order size. It was way beyond the scope of the smaller supplier. It was very likely that it would weigh it under. The buyer knew that to protect themselves, they couldn't rely on the vendor to deliver, so there was some self-interest in refusing to provide a large order. What he did do was speak candidly to this particular vendor and work with them to create a manageable situation. It was a win-win. When you are a smaller company, large orders can be like flame to a moth – attractive, but potentially lethal.

3. The Wrong Kind of Growth

Allow me a small vent on the subject of the wrong kind of growth by recalling a recent financial debacle.

On Friday, November 4, 2011, the Reuters news service issued a release touting the success of Groupon Inc.'s Initial Public Offering (IPO) of shares. It was the second largest IPO of a U.S Internet company since Google went public in 2004. Google had raised $1.7 billion; Groupon raised $700 million after only three years of being in business.

On the date of its IPO, Groupon was valued, in total, at about $13 billion. It had increased the offering by 5 million shares to 35 million in total and priced them at $20, which was above the initial range of between $16 and $18. At the time of writing, these shares, which had hit a high of $26.90, were trading at a low of $2.60, or roughly 10% of their peak value.

Groupon at its inception, in my view, was built on the wrong kind of growth. Its service, which was to offer very deeply discounted products and services to essentially what was a "buying group" of consumers, was flawed. Customers who are attracted solely by low prices are your least desirable target segment. They move from brand to brand, from product to product, with ease, driven solely by price as a discriminator. Here today and gone tomorrow. Those Groupon clients who did sign up for the "new deal" that Groupon provided got a major shock as they stood back and surveyed the carnage that was their business after the onslaught of Groupon "groupies."

I think I understand the rationale of those clients behind their decision to take on Groupon as a service. After all, the concept of sampling or discounting as a product trial is time tested and true. One issue, of course, was the size of the discount: 50% off and greater is a very sizeable discount for regular merchandise. The issues were many, of course: loss of margin, loss of regular customers, and major hits to the bottom line as the true cost of the discounting and size of the volume discounted were realized. A great deal for the consumer, not so much for the client.

And what happened? The stories of Groupon carnage got out. Clients became harder and harder to sign up. Question: Where is Groupon without any consumer offers? Answer: Nowhere. The company's concept was flawed at the outset and the company is running out of target clients to support it. The wrong kind of growth.

Let's move to a more positive story on this topic.

One of the most impactful things you can do to improve your business is to understand the profitability of your customer base. I know because I used this knowledge to triple the profitability and double the margin of a major division I was leading while *reducing* the division's revenue by 40%. Here's what we did.

After I took over the leadership of a division of a large Fortune 500 multinational, I strongly suspected not all of the division's customers were providing the kind of return we would be happy with. We hadn't done the homework to understand how much profit we were making from each of the customers. Like many earlier-stage companies, we had relied on anecdotes and gut feel. Legends had grown over time. Somehow that very large customer must be making us money because they're so large!

I asked our Finance and Sales folks to come together to analyze each of our major customers to see how profitable they were after allocating the cost of serving them to each. The analysis wasn't sophisticated, but it was close enough. The results sent a shock wave through the organization. Customers long revered turned out to be bleeding red. Others perceived to be less attractive became Belles of the Ball. We needed to take a different approach.

The first thing we did was categorize customers into three basic segments. Let's call them Gold, Silver, and Bronze. Each segment represented a different service-level, value, and return potential. Of course we didn't announce our segmentation to our customers, but we did go back to them and alter our approach.

We offered them a standard service package. On top of that service package, we created an à la carte choice of additional services that came at a further cost to them. The pricing and service could be controlled by them, which made the packaging attractive. As RFPs (Requests for Proposals) came up for bid, we would price our products and services at the level we could afford rather than use the very blunt instrument we had employed in the past. Sure we lost some bids, but we did so with the foreknowledge that if had we had priced at a level to get them, the business would have been financially unattractive. In the end, we got the right kind of business, which was transformative.

▲ ▲ ▲

We started this chapter with the premise that there is no difference between building a great business and building a business with greater value. This led us to discuss the core elements that contribute to an attractive and valuable business: core purpose, meaningful differentiation, strong people, solid infrastructure, and sustainable growth. The chapter that follows gets a little more granular in terms of the specific elements that are needed to build a resilient and valuable organization.

7
The Payoff:
Greater Business Value

I had just returned from a somewhat deflating cross-country tour, on which I had held several work sessions with business owners dealing with much of the material and focus of the first few chapters of this book. I had expected to be mobbed by each session's participants wishing to sign up for further work to help them set their company's path forward, but that didn't happen. Why?

To get an answer to that question, I turned to one of my muses, Michael Hepworth, who has always been a source of pragmatic and direct feedback. He sat and listened as I explained my situation.

"I think I understand what the issue is," he said finally. "You've done a marvelous job of providing entrepreneurs with a framework for growth. You've helped them see where they are on the organizational growth continuum and where they need to focus in order to continue growing. But you haven't told them what the payoff is for them. What's the most important thing for any business owner and entrepreneur?"

I thought about his question and replied that there was no one answer. People have intensely personal reasons for both starting and dedicating their life to building a successful business. Motivation comes in many forms. In the end, however, there is something of a scorecard for both business worth and legacy. The stronger the business, regardless of its stage of development, the greater the value. This is true whether you are looking to sell or not. And as I reflected on my experience in both running and buying and selling companies, I thought I could provide value and direction to those business owners wanting to polish their businesses regardless of whether they wanted to sell.

Michael's question inspired me to create a questionnaire that would help business owners determine the overall value of their business and provide direction for the actions they could take to drive improvement. What follows contains that questionnaire, which I have developed further and have used with many clients. I believe it can help you identify a road map to improve the value of your business. Note that it is most useful when completed by a number of individuals both inside and outside your firm. Both perspectives – outside-in as well as inside-out – are instructive.

After you've filled out the questionnaire, you'll find a detailed, question-by-question explanation of the why and how of value creation. Using this and the one page business plan tool provided in the next chapter will form the backbone of your forward action plan, with the longer-term benefit of creating a business and legacy of greater impact and value.

Imagine that you have just been hired to review the way your company conducts its business. For each question below, place an "x" beside the number that you believe most accurately reflects the state of your business today.

1 Not at all	2 To a small degree	3 To a moderate degree	4 To a large degree	5 Always

A. Business Model

1. We have good understanding of strengths/weaknesses of business.	1	2	3	4	5
2. Our business can be easily scaled.	1	2	3	4	5
3. Recurring revenue is a major portion of our business.	1	2	3	4	5
4. We are well insulated from fluctuations in market condition.	1	2	3	4	5
5. Our business has experienced several "broadsides" and survived.	1	2	3	4	5
Score					_____

B. Customer

1. No customer contributes more than 10% of returns to business.	1	2	3	4	5
2. The majority of our revenue comes from long-standing customers.	1	2	3	4	5
3. We have a deep understanding of our customers' challenges.	1	2	3	4	5
4. Our pricing initiatives, although never easy, are usually accepted.	1	2	3	4	5
5. We know our profitability and returns from each of our customers.	1	2	3	4	5
Score					_____

C. Financial Track Record

1. We have a strong cash position and mechanisms to monitor it regularly.	1	2	3	4	5
2. The company has delivered consistent revenue growth over the past three years.	1	2	3	4	5
3. Versus our competition we command and sustain a premium price.	1	2	3	4	5
4. Our bottom line margin exceeds that of the industry average.	1	2	3	4	5
5. We are well positioned to sustain our industry position and returns profile.	1	2	3	4	5
Score					

D. Leadership

1. Our CEO is deeply engaged in building the vision, goals, and strategy of the organization.	1	2	3	4	5
2. Our organization's key performance indicators are clearly outlined and measured across the business.	1	2	3	4	5
3. Our leadership team is crystal clear on the future direction of the company.	1	2	3	4	5
4. Our leadership team is aligned on the goals and direction of the business.	1	2	3	4	5
5. Our business could function effectively without the senior leadership for an extended period of time.	1	2	3	4	5
Score					

E. Differentiation/Unique Value Proposition

1. Our employees can articulate how we are uniquely different from any other company in our industry.	1	2	3	4	5
2. Our customers can define our unique point of difference.	1	2	3	4	5
3. Employees have a good understanding of company's direction.	1	2	3	4	5
4. We are crystal clear on who our customers are and why they use us.	1	2	3	4	5
5. We have mechanisms in place to gather regular customer feedback.	1	2	3	4	5
Score					

F. People systems					
1. Employee job descriptions and responsibilities are well documented.	1	2	3	4	5
2. We have a transparent compensation system tied to company goals.	1	2	3	4	5
3. We have a succession plan for the top three levels of the company.	1	2	3	4	5
4. Employee development programs are well established.	1	2	3	4	5
5. We have strong human resources support and counsel.	1	2	3	4	5
Score					

G. Product/Services					
1. Our product(s) are industry leaders.	1	2	3	4	5
2. Our product delivery processes are a source of advantage.	1	2	3	4	5
3. We have a strong development funnel of future innovation.	1	2	3	4	5
4. Our competitor benchmarking programs are well established.	1	2	3	4	5
5. We have a regular review process to optimize our product line offerings.	1	2	3	4	5
Score					

H. Planning					
1. Our company has a written annual plan used to monitor and course correct.	1	2	3	4	5
2. Plans are driven by quantitative, fact-based analysis.	1	2	3	4	5
3. Company priorities are well defined.	1	2	3	4	5
4. We have regular reviews to update plans and execution.	1	2	3	4	5
5. Plans are linked to specific, measurable projects with clear accountability.	1	2	3	4	5
Score					

I. Infrastructure

1. Financial systems are in place to get accurate insight across the business.	1	2	3	4	5
2. We have a strong demand and fulfillment forecasting system.	1	2	3	4	5
3. Our IT systems and support are solid.	1	2	3	4	5
4. Our business processes are well documented.	1	2	3	4	5
5. We have access to strong specialized resources (e.g., legal, HR, IT, Finance).	1	2	3	4	5
Score					

J. Risk Exposure

1. We have no existing or impending substantive legal challenges.	1	2	3	4	5
2. Our regulatory compliance (e.g., product, environment) is well defined.	1	2	3	4	5
3. We anticipate no substantive industry changes or challenges within five years.	1	2	3	4	5
4. We have no major investment requirements (past or future) that must be met.	1	2	3	4	5
5. Our financial base will not be under strong pressure in the next two or three years.	1	2	3	4	5
Score					

K. Contracts/Compliance

1. We have adequate insurance on all insurable property and all reasonable risk.	1	2	3	4	5
2. Contracts exist for each customer and appropriate reserves established.	1	2	3	4	5
3. We have all appropriate partnership and shareholder agreements in place.	1	2	3	4	5
4. We have no unusual long-term contractual arrangements.	1	2	3	4	5
5. Our intellectual property is well protected.	1	2	3	4	5
Score					

Total Score	

Total score of:

55–127, Red Zone: You have some heavy lifting to do before you realize the value potential of your company. Go back to the questionnaire, first by category and then by question, to build a plan of action. This is not a quick fix. It will likely take you a number of years and concerted effort to succeed. In addition to an action plan, you'll likely need some type of advisor or board to keep you on track. Think about that as a first next step.

128–201, Yellow Zone: You are partway to building the business to maximize your business value. Review your answers to the questionnaire, focusing on the areas that yielded low scores.

202–275, Green Zone: Congratulations, you have focused the business to date on most of the key drivers of value. There likely are areas that will require tweaking, but generally you are well positioned. In reviewing your questionnaire answers, prepare an action plan to address any specific areas where you indicated that the business is underperforming.

Scoring Key Commentary
A. Business Model

1. Accurate self-knowledge is perhaps the most important element in forming the base from which to develop an effective path forward. A good planning process begins with a clear understanding of the company's Strengths, Weaknesses, Opportunities, and Threats (SWOT analysis). Strengths and weaknesses describe the internal capabilities of the organization. Opportunities and threats deal with external capabilities and culpabilities. In combination they form the bedrock from which great insight is drawn and plans created. Getting it wrong means building on sand, for example, building something that

doesn't fit the organization or misfires in-market. In the early-stage company, getting it wrong likely means a quick demise.

2. Ask any venture capital or private equity shop, and they will likely cite scalability as a critical element of value. Scalability implies ease and effectiveness of growth yielding high financial return. In growth-stage parlance, the Engineer phase of an organization's growth reflects the impact of scale. In the Architect phase, the focus is on trial and experimentation, with a view to establishing a connection to the environment. It is an inherently costly and risky time in the life of an organization. Once a connection is made, the organization can focus on the connection that allows for the efficient and effective use of resources and high growth. The higher the ability of the organization to be scaled using one business model, the higher the value and faster the growth. Production of a widget is more easily scaled than a service offering. The goal should be to productize your company's offerings and reduce the amount of make to order or customized offerings to increase value.

3. Recurring revenue is desirable for many of the same reasons that being scalable is. The connection point between the two is effectiveness of effort to produce a return. It is far easier to maintain a business that has at its core a product or service that is required on an ongoing basis. Once a customer is landed, it is far easier for the company to procure another purchase. Service businesses are notorious for having business models that do not have a high percentage of recurring revenue, and they are penalized in business valuation in general for that reason. The goal of most businesses is to increase the percentage of recurring revenue.

4. The business that is well insulated from fluctuations in market conditions is also highly valued. The insulation may reflect the stability of the business or reflect the fact that the business

participates in markets that are inherently less volatile. The more predictable the returns, the higher the value.

5. A business that has experienced trauma and survived can command a higher value because it has demonstrated resilience. This resilience may come from any number of sources. The management team. The product line. The resources at its disposal. Any reason other than dumb luck adds to the attractiveness of the company. The greatest value is attributed to the company that has built fail-safe and early warning systems to sidestep or manage through adverse conditions.

B. Customer

1. Nothing should strike greater fear in a business leader's heart than a concentrated customer base. In the earlier-stage companies, particularly that of the Architect and Engineer, some concentration is to be expected. But, as the company grows, a key objective should be to diversify its customer base, spreading its risk of customer loss over that greater base. The greater the concentration, the greater the impact of customer loss and associated financial risk. And with increased risk comes a commensurate decline in corporate value and sustainability.

2. Evidence of long-standing relationships with customers also provides a risk metric. The longer the relationship (assuming a reasonable return on the customers' business), the greater the value by virtue of reduced customer flight risk. A qualitative assessment of the reason for the strength of the relationship must also be taken, however. In the case of the earlier-stage companies and service companies, in particular, the business owner/founder is often the pillar of strength and the reason the customer has been loyal. Loss of that leader or a significant change in the visibility of that leader could result in customer churn. Mechanisms to reduce the reliance on personal

relationships in favor of company-to-company relationships should be introduced. Evidence of customer churn represents either a business model that is more difficult to manage or some underlying business issues – or both.

3. Evidence of a deep understanding of customers translates to business value because it is a proxy for a good relationship. A business and leadership team that demonstrates this knowledge is on top of the business and its customers. Such a team is more likely to ward off potential threats early and also provide more value to customers because of its connection to the issues that the organization's customers are facing. To provide the greatest value, target the solution of your customers' customers' problems.

4. Your ability to execute justified price increases is a metric for the strength of your position and relationship with your customer and, in turn, your company's value. Every company encounters some push-back on executing price increases. Your ability to pass along these price increases is a strong indicator of the value – or lack of value – the customer places on your relationship. A company that has difficulty passing on pricing in a timely matter impairs its profitability and thus the value of the business.

5. Understanding your profitability by customer is a critical element in building the value of your business. This does not mean that larger, lower-margin customers are "bad" or smaller, higher-margin customers are "good." It does mean that you should segment your customer base and be strategic about the role each segment plays within your total customer profile and its effect on your business. It may be that the larger customer provides a critical role by providing volume for enhanced efficiency. A broad number of firms knowingly utilize this type of bedrock customer to keep the lights on and the machine

running even though they may be less profitable than others. Likewise, they may accept the effort/return trade-off of smaller customers if those customers' profitability is viewed as average across the customer base. The flip side may also exist. Sometimes the smaller customer requires more effort to support and is less profitable. The exercise of understanding the profitability of your customer base and segmenting it accordingly will greatly enhance your returns and sales effort.

C. Financial Track Record

1. A strong cash position and the mechanisms to monitor it are a self-evident link to company value. Strong and predicable cash flow = high value and vice versa. Planning is also a key element. It is critical to know and plan for extraordinary cash needs in high-growth phases or when taking on new customers. Many businesses are torpedoed by plummeting cash positions when they bite off more than they can chew with new customers. Sometimes "no" is absolutely the right answer even when the revenue growth and a customer look attractive. In general, the earlier the growth stage a company is in, the more focused and regular the reviews of cash should be. Weekly, if not daily, early on in the company's life.

2. Predictable, sustained growth is the objective. This type of growth is easier to plan for and manage. It improves the organization's ability to execute, which drives its value up. A company that exhibits wild swings in revenue and earnings should cause weak knees and caution among the ranks of business leadership and those reviewing the business from the outside-in. Variability in performance is a strong signal of deeper issues even when they can be explained away. Sustained, predictable growth usually heralds lower risk and greater operational effectiveness and thus higher value.

3. The ability to sustain a premium price is proof you have value in the eyes of the market and your customers. Few companies can compete in the low price segment of the market on a sustained basis. Discounting and low pricing are usually the tactics of a company that lacks a differentiated position or is in trouble. If a company is to successfully employ pricing as a primary point of difference, it must command long-term cost advantages vs. other market entrants. The street is littered with companies that thought they had a sustainable cost advantage, only to be proven wrong by competition. If you are dealing with a commoditized market or offering, your task is to determine how to break out of that situation. If you command a premium, the question is how to sustain it.

4. Another important test of superior market performance, position, and ultimately value is the degree to which you can sustain higher bottom-line margins than the industry average and your competitors. The higher the premium, the more attractive you are as a market entrant and likely the more differentiated your product and/or operational effectiveness.

5. Being able to sustain your leading industry position and returns profile reflects an adept management group and company. You likely have a strong record of growth and innovation and have robust operating systems and procedures. The combination of all of the foregoing will greatly enhance both company value and prospects for continued growth.

D. Leadership

1. The key role of CEOs is to build the vision, goals, and strategy for their business. These leaders should be out in front of their organization, spending most of their time planning and directing vs. doing the work of the organization. Organizations that are having difficulty "getting to the next level" need look

only as far as the corner office to spot the real problem. The founder/CEO has not progressed to a level of leadership competence that allows him or her to let go and delegate the operational portion of the business. Instead, such founders/CEOs remain *in* the business, driving down the value of the organization.

2. "What gets measured gets done." Generally speaking, the greater the use of appropriate metrics to evaluate and course correct, the greater the organization's business value. The use of robust metrics and infrastructure to drive the business is reflective of more sophisticated business practice. Value is increased not only because of the improved decision-making processes, but also because a strong measurement-intensive culture represents less risk in a transition process.

3. One of the strongest measures of an organization's value is its clarity of purpose and direction. A clear view of the company's direction on the part of the leadership team is critical to maintaining and building growth and momentum. The existence of obvious rifts or lack of clarity among leaders concerning company direction heralds issues both in ongoing operations and any future transition.

4. A key component of enhancing value is the degree to which a leadership team is aligned with the direction and the goals of the company. Lack of alignment drives down value and increases organizational roadblocks. A fractured leadership team sucks up resources and time and has a dysfunctional effect on the business, the employees, and, in the case of a full transition, the new ownership.

5. One of the key measures of the value of an organization is the degree to which the leadership is critical to its continued growth. Many service organizations, in particular, are created on the strength of the owner or partners. As they go, so goes

the company and its customers. If the organization can't function without the leadership for an extended period, it has less value to those who are thinking of acquiring it. It also may indicate that it is a less mature organization, or that it has an employee base or infrastructure that lacks the competence to drive the business forward should the leadership team be modified for any reason.

E. Differentiation/Unique Value Proposition

1. If your employees can articulate how you are uniquely different from any other company, you stand a good chance of actually being unique. The less commoditized the offering, the higher the value of the business. As was highlighted in previous chapters, having a differentiated market position is one of the core elements in sustaining a successful business and its value.

2. The truest test of a strong point of difference is whether your *customers* can define it. The clearer they are (and of course as long as it's valued), the higher the value of the business. The clarity of the business's difference enables it to command a premium price for its products and services and provides it with insulation against competitors. Having your distinctiveness validated by your customers is the only means by which you can determine whether you are, in fact, distinct. Being valued as unique from an outside-in perspective creates value. It is the only true measure of your differentiation. Boardroom "differentiation" counts for nothing.

3. Broad employee understanding of the company direction has a multiplier effect on the effectiveness of the organization. Lack of understanding promotes downtime as well as lack of focus, contributing to lower effectiveness and value. Having programs and processes in place to inform and communicate with employees is critical to maintaining strong employee

endorsement and understanding of the company's future. These programs also contribute to better decision-making and effectiveness through the workforce.

4. The concept of the target customer for your company is critical to directing the development of programming and services that meet with customer approval. You must understand with exceptional depth your primary customers while avoiding customer creep – the overwhelming desire to add customers and products and services that aren't aligned with your core value proposition. Being all things to all people is not a recipe for success despite some short-term wins. Do you know who your target customer is with great certainty? Do you know everything about them? About their needs and the problems they face? Are you providing them with solutions that solve *their* customers' problems? Do your employees have a good understanding? Better still, do you know who your demon customers are? Get rid of them to enhance your value.

5. No company should ever be surprised when it loses a customer. Regular, third-party feedback is critical to understanding not only what you're doing well, but also, more importantly, what you're not. The earlier-stage company has a much easier time maintaining a close relationship with its customer base. The larger the company, the more effort required to maintain strong customer relationships and an understanding of their needs. Regular customer feedback provides invaluable market and competitive knowledge. Optimal feedback mechanisms would combine both quantitative and qualitative reviews to provide depth and an ongoing metric to track progress over time.

1. A smooth-running ship is one that clearly documents employee roles, goals, and responsibilities and ensures that they are understood by all. This starts at the top, with understanding the distinct role of the CEO and the leadership team. Clear job specs and leadership competencies by management level should be developed and reviewed on a regular basis (at a minimum, annually). In earlier-stage companies, employees wear many hats and work flows to those willing to accept the responsibility to get it done. Often the founder feels responsible to play all the instruments in the band. As the company progresses in size and complexity, the work of the organization must be delegated not only more broadly but also more specifically as tasks become more specialized. The organization must walk a fine line between over- and under-staffing as it grows, maintaining the right amount of flexibility and procedural effectiveness by growth stage.

2. Employees' understanding of how they are to be compensated for their work, along with clear goals tied to compensation levels, is a minimum requirement of higher-performing companies. This underscores the need for business planning and the setting of company and, subsequently, employee annual goals. The great majority of earlier-stage companies lack both the planning regimen and discipline that yield accountability from their employees. Introducing this discipline is a prerequisite for a company to run smoothly. The sooner, the better.

3. A succession plan is critical for any business that expects to maintain its course in the face of unexpected leadership change. Unfortunately, the great majority of owner/founder-led businesses lack such a plan. Annual reviews of the succession plan for all key positions in the company are key to employee longevity and the company's ability to survive the exit of

some key employees. The reviews are also an important way to identify areas of both leverage and potential harm and are a mechanism for dealing with each. Clear succession planning is a further indication of good management and thus improves the prospects of enhanced business performance and survival.

4. The movement from Architect to the more complex business system evidenced in the Conductor stage requires a progression of sophistication with respect to the skills of the employee base. What got you there, in an earlier-stage company, won't get you there in a more complex organization. For a company to progress through the stages of growth, the employee skill base must grow as well. Some of this will be acquired through the injection of skills and employees brought in from the outside. Many employees will require further development to keep pace with the new requirements of the later-stage company. A well-developed and well-formulated employee development plan not only is key to continued growth but also yields benefits in both employee effectiveness and loyalty. It also acts as a filter to identify which employees are best able to contribute to organizational growth and which aren't.

5. Mention Human Resources to an earlier-stage company owner and you are likely to get a strong reaction – negative. For good reason. The earlier-stage company shouldn't focus a lot of effort in this area other than to rent advice and counsel that is appropriate to its stage of business and employee complexity. As the company's employee base grows, the need for employee support, systems, and processes grows as well. In terms of timing, HR audits should be sought from HR generalists as the company builds to the Engineer stage. It is important with earlier-stage companies to ensure regulatory compliance at minimum. As the company grows, it will require more frequent and broader-based management competency and HR systems development.

1. It goes without saying that owning the leadership position with your products and services is a source of value to your organization. To the leader go the spoils. Higher returns and growth. The goal of your organization, regardless of its growth stage, must be to represent, in the eyes of your most important customer target, the leading position. This last sentence has been crafted with care. Leadership is defined by your customers, not the people sitting in your boardroom or around the office. Too many companies and owner/founders are culpable of believing their own press – or worse, of not listening when their customers speak.

2. A product or service can create value and differentiation simply in the way it is delivered. Amazon is a good example of a total business that was solely built on a delivery process. The effectiveness of your go-to-market business system plays a very large part in your total value equation. First, it has cost implications. Regular reviews should be taken across your industry and competition to ensure that your systems are running efficiently and effectively. Cost savings identified and returned here can create resources for redeployment for advancement elsewhere or added to the bottom line. Second, it is something that is susceptible to revision for advantage. Competitive reviews can provide you with an early warning system of the need to innovate or of an opportunity to innovate.

3. Growth requires innovation whether it's a goal of the company to continue progressing through growth stages or not. A strong funnel of innovation is critical to survival because the competitive landscape is constantly changing. When considering innovation, many overlook the opportunity to innovate processes as well as products. Returning quickly to our S curve model from chapter 1, the most effective time to introduce

the seeds of innovation is when the company is experiencing growth. This is when the company's resources and risk profile are best suited to allow for experimentation and failure.

4. In much of the business literature, competitive knowledge and market intelligence are cited as a core competence of the successful company. Regular reviews of the competitive landscape and your company's performance within that landscape are key to continued growth and prosperity. This type of review is less formal and ritualized in the Architect and Engineer stages. The earlier-stage company does face a greater danger of anecdotal competitive reviews and needs to guard against them. Thriving companies regularly seek feedback and spend resources to monitor the environment in which they compete. Because they build competitor and market insight, they are better able not only to defend threats but also to be proactive, accessing opportunities sooner.

5. Products and service line offerings require care and feeding even if they have had long lives and good in-market success. Trends in profitability, revenue, and market position offer good clues to the vitality and strength of your offerings. Optimizing your products or services often means introducing smaller innovations or line-up modifications to remain current and vibrant. And new isn't the only opportunity. A well-timed elimination of a product or service can also yield substantial benefit to your overall organizational effectiveness and competitive position.

H. Planning

1. The discipline of creating and using a written plan to monitor and course correct is rare among the vast majority of earlier-stage companies. Some studies report as few as 1% of companies with 100 employees or fewer utilize a formal planning process. Other studies reveal that those who plan outperform those who

don't by over 40%. Businesses that take a disciplined approach to building their businesses are better able to both anticipate and manage through the rough patches. The value ascribed to those companies who plan is also commensurately higher than that of their brethren who do not. A strong case for planning.

2. The lack of systems and reporting mechanisms in the earlier-stage companies is often associated with management-by-anecdote. Feedback mechanisms are drawn from the experience and views of employees regarding the marketplace or from kitchen-table discussions. As companies mature and grow in complexity, they must rely more directly on data and the insight that can be drawn from the data for decision-making and policy development. The use of metrics to drive operational effectiveness and efficiency is the hallmark of a firm that is moving toward sophistication. The late Conductor stage of corporate growth sees this practice turn in on itself. Often, companies in the throes of decline or stagnation will enter a stage of "the perpetual plan." Annual plans beget quarterly plans that beget weekly and sometimes even daily planning supported by legions of bureaucrats. This is when planning becomes counterproductive, acting as a barrier to action and hastening the downward spiral to the Renovator stage, when the very survival of the firm is at stake.

3. The scourge of any company at any stage of development is misdirection of effort and resources. The process of creating well-articulated and communicated priorities is one of the most important at any level of corporate size or development. The earlier-stage company is often guilty of having the priorities locked in the owner/founder's mind (which is prone to sudden change). Employees are left guessing or second-guessing the owner in trying to determine forward action. The best-laid projects are simple, clear, few, and strictly prioritized.

4. Every solid planning effort must be attended by a regular review process to ensure that what was intended to happen actually happens. These reviews are the backbone of the company's ability to course-correct and drive accountability through the organization. Planning without the discipline of regular review and modification undermines the benefit.

5. A key fault found in many planning systems is lack of specificity around project parameters and accountability. A project's intended outcome and path forward must be both discussed and agreed by the appropriate management group to balance the resources required to complete the project against the benefit. Also required is specificity of project ownership. One and only one name should appear as owner of the project. Of course many may contribute, but true accountability exists when one person is responsible.

I. Infrastructure

1. Strong financial systems and the right people to populate the finance arena is arguably the most important pillar for the growing company. As companies move through the Architect and Engineer stages, they can usually get by with a controller or bookkeeper. The move toward a larger and more complex organization requires a bedrock of information from which insight concerning every area of the company's operation can be drawn. It is usually in the Engineer or Conqueror stage that the old financial system, usually jury-rigged over time, finally reveals its shortcomings. The move to a more comprehensive ERP (Enterprise Resource Program) is sought. This alone can be a monumental blow to both company and the employee base. The addition of an individual with CFO skills and acumen is also needed at this stage of development, or earlier if possible. This individual usually provides a complement to

the owner/founder. Every Captain Kirk needs a Spock. In this case, the system and personnel can provide the much-needed discipline and attention to the day-to-day management of the business while allowing the entrepreneur to do what he or she does best – build.

2. A strong demand and fulfillment forecasting system is important to help smooth the company's operations as it fulfills customer requirements. It also acts as an early warning mechanism of the need for a surge in capacity or a change of course in the case of a shortfall in demand. Historical and customer data associated with these systems can also be instrumental in identifying new opportunity areas.

3. With the introduction of the personal computer and Internet, IT has moved in importance from background to foreground. Strong advances in applications dedicated to the smaller, earlier-stage company have set the stage for marked improvement in performance vs. history. Off-the-shelf ERP systems have also provided much-needed support for the early-stage company. ERP systems are a double-edged sword, as anyone who has survived an SAP conversion can attest. On the upside, they provide a solid time- and market-tested infrastructure for the burgeoning company. On the downside, they can disrupt culture and process with an attendant downfall in business performance. The move to more sophisticated systems can be a significant draw on the resources of a company and must be timed correctly.

4. It is relatively easy to describe the processes associated with the early-stage company. There are none. Everything is new so everything is created from first principles. As the company develops into the Engineer and Conqueror stages and moves toward predictability, there is an increasing need across the organization to document process. Developing process is not

usually an entrepreneurial strength. Process is necessary to build consistency into the organization and enable the organization to streamline its use of resources – both its employees and the systems themselves. A company that demonstrates solid, documented process is better able to sustain its performance through periods of upheaval and yields better returns. It is also able to sustain itself distinct from leadership of the company.

5. With the move to a more complex organization comes the requirement of a more specialized and deeper skill base in all key functional areas. The earlier-stage company should rent as need arises. Acquiring the type of individual and skills needed for later-stage companies would be overkill for an earlier-stage company and also outstrip its resources. The more advanced the stage of a company, the greater its need of deeper skills in each of the functional areas. Adding these skills is a fine balancing act of need, costs, and benefits.

J. Risk Exposure

1. It should be intuitively obvious that, from a valuation perspective, existing or impending legal challenges increase the risk associated with the business and thus reduce company value. In certain cases, however, a company should address a challenge in order to protect intellectual property and corporate reputation. In select instances, this will be seen by prospective purchasers not as an extra cost but as added value.

2. Regulatory compliance is an area that frequently gets overlooked in an earlier-stage company. In many cases, it is not a lack of foresight but lack of knowledge that is the culprit. What you don't know can hurt you regardless of your business size. Compliance audits should be considered and performed periodically to ensure that the company is not exposed to this

type of risk and to remain knowledgeable about regulatory guidelines, which frequently change.

3. An industry that has demonstrated volatility, or one for which substantive change is expected, creates uncertainty and risk. Linked to a planning initiative, a regular review of industry dynamics is critical in planning and implementing future initiatives and reducing commensurate risk to the business. The introduction of this discipline and the foresight that it provides positions the company better to meet the anticipated change.

4. As discussed earlier, there are pinch points in an organization's growth that will require investment and recapitalization. The timing of expenditures to support growth is a delicate balance. The type and focus of the investments will also vary by business and industry vertical. For example, service businesses are highly sensitive to investment in people, and manufacturing to capital expenditure. When and how to invest is one of the more difficult questions to ask and answer because in many circumstances the investment itself is required to support growth, which may or may not come about. A business facing the imminent need for some kind of investment or capital infusion is inherently a higher-risk proposition and thus commands a lower value.

5. Corporate growth is not linear. It occurs in fits and starts as the company moves through the stages of growth. Any condition that presages financial pressure, whether externally or internally generated, increases risk and thus diminishes value. Again, demonstration of corporate knowledge and plans to address these situations reduce the perception of an organization's risk.

1. This is an area that can get overlooked in the earlier-stage company. In the chaos of activity in the Architect growth stage, insurance is often an oversight. Even for a later-stage company, reviews of the adequacy of insurance coverage and policy premiums should be undertaken regularly. Given the changing landscape of the insurance industry in general, a company may be pleasantly surprised by lower costs, which make the review process more palatable.

2. Because of its close ties to its customer base, the earlier-stage company is more susceptible to doing business on a handshake. Regardless of size, contracts should exist for each customer engagement. Period. The streets are littered with the corpses of companies that trusted and lost. Contracts provide a paper trail, which is a legal necessity for companies at all stages. They also help later-stage companies in their financial analysis and development of solid business systems.

3. Nobody who falls in love and marries feels at the outset that the marriage will falter. Partnerships and shareholder agreements are unfortunately a must for all businesses regardless of growth stage. Despite this advice, the great majority of companies at the Architect and Engineer stages have inadequate or no documentation to support ownership. Those that choose to continue to do business this way are at very real personal and professional risk.

4. Earlier-stage companies that have close relationships with their customers and clients often run the risk of creating "unique" circumstances and relationships. These relationships, important in the throes of building a company and market position, can cause headaches for the company as it moves to maturity. Scrutiny across the variety of business relationships increases

from customer and regulatory agencies alike as the company grows. Dealing with these situations earlier in the company's growth yields a smoother sail in the later stages and also reduces the risk of business loss or legal action.

5. The need to protect intellectual property and the diligence with which this is approached vary by company and industry. In general, a company is more highly valued in relationship to the strength and protection of its IP. The more critical and distinct the IP to your company and its future, the more important it is to protect it.

Using the Questionnaire

I realize that this has been a particularly heavy chapter. In some ways it is an encapsulation of best practices for businesses, especially for those at the Conductor stage of business development. For businesses in earlier-growth cycles, certain activities, including focusing on the development of infrastructure, are impractical and, frankly, not affordable. Use the questionnaire as a guide to help you identify the priority actions that, over time, will drive your organization's business improvement.

I've now worked with the questionnaire over several years and with many companies and have received some valuable in-field learning. To maximize the value of the tool for you, I reiterate that respondents to it should come from as broad a base as possible, from inside and, if possible, outside your company. Capturing both an inside and outside perspective often yields some surprising differences. For obvious reasons, it should also be administered and tabulated in complete confidence. Respondents should be encouraged to complete the questionnaire when they are able to focus on the task on hand.

Insight is provided both question by question and also across various audiences (e.g., CEO/business owner perspective vs.

leadership team perspective). **By far the greatest value of the tool is the team dialogue that is generated when the results are reviewed.** This offers an opportunity to talk about key strengths and opportunity areas for the company. Through that discussion, priority action can be determined, with the side benefit of improving team alignment and focus on the task(s) at hand. It provides a strong base from which to move on to the next part of the program – developing the plan.

▲ ▲ ▲

All of the foregoing has paved the way for me to present you with the world's best business tool. Read on!

8

The World's Best Business Tool: Your One Page Plan

You're about to learn about a great business tool to transform your business and create the accountability that will get you out of working *in* your business to working *on* your business. It's versatile and scalable. I've used it to drive business integrations in the billions of dollars and to help many business owners transform their small- and medium-sized businesses. It's simple, straightforward, and extremely powerful. It's your one page plan.

Before we begin, I need to ask you two questions. First, do you have a written business plan? And second, do you use it?

It's usually at this stage of my conversations with business owners that I start to hear the crickets chirping. They mumble something about having one but not really using it, or once having had one. Other reactions include:

- "They're too much effort, and we wouldn't use it anyway"

- "Planning takes time away that I could be spending on my business"

- "The plans just end up gathering dust on a shelf"

- "We already know what we have to do. There's no point in wasting time writing it down"

- "We're too small to need a plan"

- "I just haven't gotten around to it"

- "I've never found these business plans remotely useful"

- "I don't know how to do it"

- "We already have one: it's called our budget"

You might be shocked to find out that under 1% of all the business owners I speak to have a written plan, much less use one. If you don't have one, you are in, by far, the majority. However, stick with me here, and by the end of this chapter you'll have a terrific tool to help you build and focus your business activity. The key to its effectiveness will be the extent to which you keep it at the center of day-to-day execution. A great tool unused is the same as no tool at all.

The Business Case for Planning

My previous life was spent working in a monolithic firm, the leaders of which seemed to spend all of their time planning and re-planning. One wonders when they actually had time to *do*. Since then, however, I've seen the benefits of planning much closer up. They are transformational, and, perhaps surprisingly, this is particularly so for smaller businesses. Following are just some of the benefits I've seen in businesses over the last ten years of my advisory work, particularly with small- and medium-sized enterprises.

- Stronger and more robust top-line growth

- Accountability

- Enhanced bottom-line performance

- Improved alignment and common focus

- Commonly understood key objectives and deliverables

- Improved resource allocation

- More clearly defined operating and project priorities

- Identification of high-level key challenges

- Establishment of an early warning system

While these are all wonderful things, by far the biggest benefit to leaders of businesses is getting their life back. Good planning streamlines and builds a system of accountability that gives everyone more freedom. When people understand where they're headed, they can take personal responsibility to help get there and also feel better and more engaged as a result. What's not to like?

The One Page Plan Overview

Your one page plan has three sections:

- *The top section* is for describing, in a few words, your company destination. I'll describe how to identify and place this "stake in the ground" in a moment.

- *The middle section*, placed directly under the destination, is for your choice of metrics to determine whether you're making progress toward that destination. The metrics are the three to five things you believe critical to measure your progress toward your destination. For example, Revenue, Margin, and Cash.

- *The bottom section* contains the specific actions that you will focus on in moving toward your destination. This includes the timing and persons accountable for those actions.

Put these three sections together, and you have a concise document that will help transform and drive your business forward. Here's the format. (See Appendix 2 for a sample of a filled-out plan.)

Figure 8.1 – Sample One Page Plan

DESTINATION

Key Performance Indicators (KPIs)
- Revenue Growth
- EBITDA
- Cash Flow
- Productivity

Build Top Line Growth

Action	Who?	Timing

Build Manufacturing Capability

Action	Who?	Timing

Build People Resources

Action	Who?	Timing

Build Customer Experience

Action	Who?	Timing

Improve Core Business Processes

Action	Who?	Timing

I walked into a cocktail party a few years back and was introduced to somebody I hadn't met before. During the course of the conversation, he asked me a simple question.

"Where are you taking your company?"

The answer I gave was my destination statement, a concise statement of the desired end goal for my company, using lay terms he could understand.

Many planning exercises start with building vision, mission, and core values statements. While the discussions held when building these are generally fruitful, they lack, for me at least, the most important test – clear communication. The examples I've seen are often wrapped in "business or strategy speak." I can't imagine replying to a cocktail party question with a company vision or mission.

In his great book *The Art of the Start*, Guy Kawaguchi writes at length about his experiences with lengthy vision and mission statements. In some of his YouTube appearances, he spends time demonstrating the "Dilbert Mission Statement Generator." You know things have gone too far when there's a cartoon software app that allows you to press a button and generate a ready-made mission statement. They sound great and say absolutely nothing.

That's why I believe the idea of a destination statement is many times more effective. Every business needs to put a stake in the ground so employees understand the goal line. That's the destination statement. It's the answer to the question, "Where are we going?"

Following are three examples of effective destination statements.

"Big Enough to Move"

One of my former clients, Tony, a business owner of a small food manufacturing facility, had started the process of building a business plan. Like most small businesses, this one had no plan, written or otherwise. It just "did." Tony had grown up in a much larger company and thought he would bring some best practices of the larger firm to the organization. To kick-start the process, he spent time on his own to develop draft vision, mission, and values statements for the company. His thought was that, rather than having key employees build these from the ground up, he would share his and ask for their suggestions. (Just as an aside, group writing is usually a very painful, negative experience. He was right to create something for people to push against. Much, much more effective.)

Tony booked a full morning for his key employees to review his work and give him their input. During the meeting, he spent about an hour reviewing his rationale for the statements. When he asked for input, a lone hand was raised by one of his hourly workers at the back of the room. With some trepidation, the employee stood up and addressed the room.

"I don't know about all those fancy words. I look around this place that we call an office and I think we've got one thing to focus on. To get big enough to move!"

And with that, he sat down.

Whoa! To his credit, Tony really listened. He reflected on what had been said and concluded that he'd just been handed a gem. "Big enough to move" could be both a rallying cry and a destination. It was something that connected with all of them and was aspirational. To his credit, he turned his whole agenda upside down and began with that statement as the destination. He and his team spent the rest of the time talking about what it meant to be "big enough to move" and then what they needed to do to get there. Brilliant!

In another case, I was working with a company on the West Coast. This was a larger company, in the hundreds-of-millions-of-dollars-in-revenue kind of way. Same scenario. No written plan. I introduced the idea of a destination statement and the need for simplicity this way.

"Imagine that you've just arrived at cocktail party and somebody has come over to speak with you. After the initial pleasantries, they ask about your business and where you plan to take it over the next couple of years. Your answer to that person, who doesn't know your business (or perhaps doesn't even care about it), should be a destination statement. A paragraph answer won't do. It's got to be short, sweet, and easily understood. With no numbers!

That's another dirty little secret, by the way. Your employees really don't give a rat's you know what about the numbers. Nor does that person at the cocktail party. They care about how the company relates to them and/or how it makes them feel. People get connected at the emotional, not the rational, level.

This client had a service business that was expanding internationally. When the dust cleared, the destination statement, as written and talked about was, "To own the global [insert service line] business."

My lawyer friends might have some competition-law issues with that statement, but it was motivating. Once we'd put the stake in the ground, building the plan was easy.

"Third Graders"

The last example of a destination statement is my retelling of a story from the book *Switch* by Chip and Dan Heath. I love this story because it brings home that we use and are motivated by destination statements long before we realize it.

The story involves a teacher who arrived at the beginning of September to a brand new grade one class. This was the first year that she'd taught, and the class was particularly unruly that first day. She thought that night about her experience and landed on something she thought she'd try at the beginning of the next day.

When she arrived the next morning she wrote in big bold chalk letters. "3rd Graders by the end of this year!" Once seated, she explained herself.

"Class, what I've written on the board is something that I think you'll all be excited about."

Then she shared with them that they could learn enough that year to reach the level of kids in grade three. The kids' eyes widened and chatter erupted. Third graders! Wow! Then the questions started firing.

"How? What do we need to do? Can you really think we can do it?"

That teacher was some smart lady!

I know that, for many of us, our memories of grade one are fading. The one thing I do remember is how I used to feel about third graders. They were ancient! And smart! And strong! They were so far out of my league that I thought I'd never get there.

That teacher created all of these feelings with her destination statement. Wow! Imagine how effective this approach could be for your business.

Building the Destination Statement

The power and quality of your business plan will be driven by the power and quality of your destination statement. It's the stake you drive into the ground in front of your organization so they can see where they're going. It must be emotive and inspiring. Your employees will determine whether they sign up or sign out based on it. You'll know when you've nailed a destination statement. It resonates. It feels right, and those who read it will tell you so.

So how to create your destination statement? Truth is, even as I railed against the concept of a "vision," the destination statement is somewhat similar. For many, the statement is the reason they built a business in the first place. They saw opportunity to change the game that was being played, or they saw an improvement that they could bring to market. Simply identifying that opportunity for change could provide the foundation of a great destination statement.

For example, one of the service companies I work with describes their destination as "changing the way the market feels about the [insert type of service] we provide." Sony had a great destination statement that drove it to greatness: "To change the world's view of Japanese products as being inferior." For those of us who aren't old enough to remember Japanese products after World War Two, they faced a similar situation to some Chinese companies today. Most of the products were of inferior quality and were known to be. Imagine how inspiring it must have been for those Japanese employees to work for a company that was going to bring themselves and their country back to worldwide recognition and respectability! Great stuff.

I encourage you, as you create your destination statement, to review both where you've come from and what you believe to be your core strengths or opportunities. You would do well to make this a "From – To" exercise in which you juxtapose where you're coming "from" in terms of history and competency against where you're heading "to."

Building the Action Plan

Let me jump to consider the third section of your one page plan. This section houses the actions, accountability, and timing that you develop for your business plan. The actions you identify will become the work of the business. These are the specific plans that you believe are critical to making progress to your destination. They are the priority projects, above the regular work of the company.

An old boss of mine sat me down one day and taught me a great lesson about establishing and managing priorities.

"Imagine that you've got an empty glass in front of you," he said. "That glass represents the organization. Next to the glass is a number of marbles with each of the marbles representing key projects that the organization could undertake. It's pretty obvious that the glass will only house a fraction of the marbles available.

"Your job is twofold. The first, and probably the most important, part is to determine which marbles should be placed in the glass. The glass, like the company, is capable of holding only so many marbles, so you better pick the right ones. The second part is to make sure that the glass is always full of the most important marbles, because there are always new marbles available. You've also got to remember that if one marble goes in, another marble has to come out. There's only so much room in the glass."

In order to populate your plan with your priority actions, consider using a two-phase approach. To fast-forward the process, assign homework to be completed prior to a planning meeting. Ask each participant to outline the three to five most important strategic projects for their area in the coming year. This will make it easier for you, at the planning meeting, to build and vet a collective list of priority actions.

High-priority activities, on a company-wide basis, most often can be fit in five broad thrusts or categories.

Growth

Growth initiatives include major new products or services. M&A initiatives, and so on. The reason to group them is to provide focus and priority. These are your big bets.

People

People drive the activity and thus the business. The actions will include major initiatives as they relate to building your human resource base and competencies.

Major activities related to sales and marketing.

Product/service lines and processes.

These are the bedrock systems projects: Finance, IT, Legal, and so on.

Once you've identified the individual projects, add one name for each as the project lead and the timing. Ideally, the company owner/CEO name should not appear anywhere on the project list. This forces accountability and delegation into the organization. For examples of key projects, see Appendix 3.

Establishing the Metrics

Now let's go back and consider the middle section of your one page plan.

As Stephen Covey puts it, "What gets measured, gets done." So true! It doesn't matter whether you're talking about dieting, business, or marks in school. Simply maintaining a measurement system improves your execution. Also important is what gets measured.

I spent a fair bit of my early career in a large organization. Every year I dreaded the review process, both for myself and those who reported to me. Each year a portion of time would be set aside to "reflect" with your superior on the accomplishments of the prior year. The reality was that the better you pitched your review performance, the better your reward at the end of the year in terms of your bonus and pay increment. The problem with the system was that, in addition to more than a little "credit stealing" that went on, there was a tendency to substitute quantity for quality. I really didn't look forward to my reports coming to me with the forty things they had achieved over the last year when most of those things were inconsequential.

Probably too late in the game, I happened to hit on a solution. I reflected that the reality of how I was rating people was how they performed on the one to three really big projects over the year. Why not determine these projects up front, focus on them for the year, and measure them throughout the year so there are no surprises when review time comes? That would do away with the post-game performance sales pitches and provide a great way to measure progress along the way. It certainly would be much better than having forty priorities either before or after the fact. I met with each employee at the beginning of the year and agreed on what mattered. From there it was simple. If something became more important (remember the glass and the marbles), one thing came out and it went in. It worked beautifully!

The measurements you use to drive your one page plan should be viewed with similar importance. My advice is to limit your measurement to as few elements as possible, never more than five. These are your company's areas of focus. They are what you will hold your employees individually and collectively accountable. Doing so will increase alignment and focus. What you choose to measure is up to you. Measurement criteria will vary to some extent, but my preference is to have a measurement proxy for at least the following:

- Growth (e.g., Revenue)

- Business Quality (e.g., EBITDA margin)

- Business Sustainability (Cash Flow)

For examples of possible metrics, see Appendix 4, Sample Key Performance Indicators. Bottom line: stitch together the three elements of company destination, metrics to measure progress to that destination, and the actions you'll focus on to get there and you will have your one page plan. See Appendix 2 for a sample of a one page plan.

Further Thoughts on Planning

Much, if not all, of the answer is already known to the organization. How many times have you heard the lament that the majority of consultants just mine information that already exists in the company and parrot it back? To some degree that's true. The collective knowledge of any team is a powerful thing, and the sheer number of years of industry and business experience represented by a planning group is usually impressive. It's also almost always more focused than any outside resource. In my experience, the key to good planning is not an exercise in new thought, it's the discovery and unlocking of information that's already held.

The answer, my friends, is not blowing in the wind – it's been with you all along.

Communication and sharing are arguably the major benefits of planning. Put another way, it's as much about the journey as it is the destination. In every size and type of firm that I work in, the ability to come together and problem-solve is critical to the quality of a plan and its execution. The process allows each team player to represent his or her area of expertise while simultaneously gaining a holistic view of the others' contributions to the entire company.

The process is best facilitated by a third party. Whether the facilitator is an insider or someone contracted from outside the firm, he or she must be regarded as impartial, with no vested interest in the outcome of the exercise and no agenda to favor one particular group over another. An experienced third party facilitator can also more easily and tactfully ask certain "politically incorrect" questions while smoothing over any rough edges that emerge between people and functions. He or she can also challenge the participants to ensure that group-think doesn't take hold of the process. The last person who should ever drive the process is the CEO or owner!

Participants must understand the exercise's purpose, process, timing, and individual expectations. For participants to be fully engaged, they need full information about why this process has been developed and how it will affect them individually and collectively. Knowing this ahead of time will help them commit to the program. Without this important step, the planning process – not to mention the input and output – likely will be flawed. If possible, it is beneficial to engage an outside-in perspective (for example, from a key customer, supplier, or shareholder) to help ensure that planning input is balanced.

Communicating the proposed process ahead of time is also critical, since the participants must be able to build this new activity into their ongoing work. Setting the expectations and establishing the process in advance improves participants' commitment to the process. You can increase their commitment further by including, in advance, the opportunity for participants to provide input and ask questions.

The time set aside for the planning process must be focused and short. Most people see planning as tangential to their primary job – to execute. The greatest risk associated with planning exercises is that the process becomes unwieldy and excessively bureaucratic, eventually suffocating under its own weight. The best planning process is quick, requires minimal pre-work from the team, and results in very clear actions, time lines, and accountability.

The plan must be the focal point of the day-to-day activity of the company.

9
The Best-Laid Plans:
Sustainable Change

Breaking free of your success cage is within your reach. We've covered organizational and leadership characteristics through the life cycle of a business and driven it down to where your company is currently operating. We've provided self-analysis tools to aid you in identifying priority areas, along with a simple framework to drive your future action: the one page plan. Only one step remains. The most important step. Doing something!

There is an insidious beast between you and your goal. It is called inertia. The greatest frustration for a leader and organization is to see great work destroyed by inactivity or inaction. The simple truth is this, **unless a system is created to introduce and maintain action, a plan won't be executed**. It's no surprise that there are so many books on leading change. The strongest tendency of any body is to preserve its state of rest or carry on in a uniform direction.

Organizations are like a stubborn mule. You have to start by whacking them hard enough to get their attention. Unfortunately, that's not enough, because left to their own devices they'll just go back to what they were doing. What's needed is constant vigilance and a good whack every once in a while to get them to *continue* to pay attention and stay on the new path that has been chosen. Eventually they'll get it, but it takes a lot of energy.

A Simple Framework for Change Management

I'm going to start the discussion of change management with a personal observation drawn from many years of working with leaders and their organizations. The big learning? Impetus for change usually occurs in reaction to a major negative event or the perception of a significant imminent threat. The attraction of a wonderful, exciting future doesn't cut it as a motivator. There are very few Steve Jobs types around. Fear, real or perceived, is by far the strongest motivator in breaking inertia.

A fellow advisor and I recently shared notes on our experiences with clients. We talked specifically about succession planning. One thing that had dumbfounded both of us was the fact that very few business owners feel compelled to think about or plan for their eventual retirement despite the litany of positive benefits in doing so. The benefits of an orderly, planned exit have been well documented. It provides for a smooth transition, higher business valuation, and on and on. Our joint observation was that none of these strong, positive outcomes seemed to ignite any form of action. In the vast majority of cases, nothing was done until the proverbial you-know-what hit the fan.

Physics wasn't my strong suit in high school, but Newton's first law of motion holds some strength for me when I think about business owners and their aversion to planning or even thinking about their eventual exit plans. "A body in motion remains in motion unless it is acted on by an external force." It's the same with the business owner. My experience is that some major external event is required for a business leader and owner to act. What types of events? A health crisis. Business failure or at least significant leakage. Marital or family circumstances. Unfortunately, the attraction of a wildly promising future is very infrequently the impetus for change. It takes the realization that you are either standing in a pile of poop, or about to, to act. Necessity really is the mother of invention.

It's a sad reality is that few companies or people create impetus for change on their own. And that, in the vast majority of these situations, immediate change is required. A hurry-up offense may create excitement in football, but this type of activity in business often doesn't end well. The key learning should be self-evident. Those who plan yield a far better result on transition than those who don't. Period.

Change isn't easy. That's why the literature abounds with the subjects of change and change management. One model that appeals to me was introduced by Kurt Lewin in 1951.* He called it the "force field" framework of change. Like Newton's first law pertaining to objects, Lewin describes organizations as systems that are held in equilibrium by equal and opposing forces. The forces are divided between those sponsoring change (e.g., new technology, competitive incursions) and those resisting change (e.g., business practices, culture).

Lewin's framework describes change as a three-step process. As you review the following, I encourage you to draw the analogy to your business.

Step 1: Unfreeze (Break Inertia)

Lewin observes that change will not occur unless there is motivation in the organization to do so. The force for change must be greater than that which resists it. He goes on to add that change involves not only new learning but the process of *unlearning* habits and processes. This last point bears underscoring. What got you here won't get you there!

The leadership of the organization and the organization itself must unlearn some of the practices that made them successful in

---

* Lewin, Kurt. *Field Theory in Social Science: Selected Theoretical Papers.* New York: Harper & Row, 1951.

the first place. For the leader and entrepreneur, it's very simple: **You have to establish the goal and then let go and let the organization do the work**. All of the leaders I have worked with who have broken free of the cage had to learn this one very tough lesson. If you don't, you won't break free. Robert was lucky that he learned the importance of delegation early in his tenure as a new partner in a mid-sized accounting firm. Here's what he wrote me:

> Delegate, delegate, delegate. Never do yourself what you've hired others to do.
>
> When I started out in my firm, nobody was working harder than I was. In fact, I couldn't figure out why others seemed to have more time and seemed less stressed. One day the senior partner pulled me aside and gave me some advice that I have used to this day.
>
> "The value you provide to the organization is in providing leadership and direction," he told me, "not in doing the work of the organization. Your job is to help find the resources to make the company run better and to be the key link to the outside world."
>
> I doubt that my business or my life would be nearly as successful had I not been given that advice many years ago. I owe a debt of gratitude to that senior partner that I hope to repay to those coming up behind me.

Beyond the leader's inability or unwillingness to delegate, inertia is perhaps the most difficult obstacle to overcome. The organization must support the direction. It must need the change to occur and believe that it will. Most change initiatives are undermined by actions, not words. The business owner falls back into old habits. Change initiatives are not supported with consistency. The list goes on and on. It doesn't take much to derail the initiative. Perhaps this is precisely why it takes a major – and usually negative – external event not only to underscore the need for change but also to exert the consistent reinforcement needed to keep the change on course.

Once inertia has been broken and a direction has been established and the first steps have been taken, the direction must be supported from the top. Here's a quick story to illustrate just how critical top-level support is to sustaining momentum.

My colleague and I were asked to fly to Portugal to present our credentials and review a key project for one of the world's largest communication companies. The project was to redefine and embellish this company's customer experience.

We got our first hint of impending disaster when a presentation outlining the company goals was sent to us ahead of time.

Allow me a quick vent here. I can't stand corporate-speak! Especially buzzwords and those who use them. I'd like to string up all those who have read the latest *Harvard Business Review* article and feel compelled to use the latest bafflegab on the rest of us to prove how smart they are – even if they really don't get it. Few would convict me, I think, if I did away with anyone who used BHAG again (Big Hairy Audacious Goal). There, I'm done. Back to our story.

The presentation sent to us had been populated with every buzzword then known about customer experience. Phrases like "delighting the customer" and "exceeding customer expectations" were thrown about with gay abandon. It was clearly written to appease the corporate gods. "It must be a great project! Look at all the fancy words and concepts we've managed to weave together!"

We got our second hint of disaster when we arrived at the corporation's head office. We had just flown from North America via London to Lisbon with three or four hours of sleep at best before we were shown into the boardroom. We looked around the room. Not one executive in the place! Not one! The highest-ranking person was the person who supposedly had commissioned the project (a first-line manager). She had assured us that the project was a critical initiative and was supported broadly by those at the highest level of the organization, all of whom would be attending the meeting.

Crickets started chirping. I looked at my partner. He looked at me. It was over before it began. No executive interest. No change. Period. We parted ways, wishing them the best but resigned to the project's failure. We fired the client. In the aftermath, we heard that it bumped along for a while, fizzled, and then died. How many change initiatives die for the same reason? In my experience, a lot!

What do the organizational development experts say are the strongest methods to provide the impetus for change? To paraphrase, they are:

- Use a stick

- Use a treat

- Use both

And two additional thoughts from yours truly.

- Make it personal. Bring the benefit down to the individual level. Nobody really cares about the company. They care about what happens to them

- Be consistent and relentless

Step 2: Change

Or, to put it another way, adjust the equilibrium toward new activity. Add accountability and measurement.

The experts cite several ways to ensure that change is introduced and supported.

One is to form a leadership coalition. Start first with leadership. Get buy-in and make them accountable for the change initiative with clear roles and responsibilities.

Another is to create a compelling end state. Again, this comes down to the personal level. "I may understand the end state for the company, but if I don't buy in at the 'me' level, you don't own my heart."

Yet another is to build momentum with short-term wins. Too often, leaders feel compelled to throw a Hail Mary pass. Every good quarterback and coach knows the importance of putting points on the board, but they also know that most often that happens incrementally. One of the most effective ways to build momentum is to create and celebrate the small wins. Successes that come frequently build belief and support for change initiatives.

Step 3: Re-freeze

Institutionalize the new approaches and new rules, rewards, and measurement.

Beyond Theory: The Process and Some Additional Tools

Ask weight-loss clinics for the key ingredient to their clients' success and you'll get a very consistent answer: Staying with the program. Unfortunately, the vast majority of us can't be trusted to rely on ourselves alone to stay the course over the long haul. We need a drill instructor. Someone who will be our conscience, provide outside-in feedback, and make us accountable over the longer term. My experience is that, in the vast majority of cases, leaders who are able to break free of their success cage put someone in place to act as that instructor.

Performing the role of drill instructor, particularly for the entrepreneur, is not for the faint of heart. Remember the Big Five Psychological Factors of Entrepreneurship? We discussed them in chapter 3 as risk tolerance, self-reliance, openness to new ideas, persistence, and extroversion. It takes a very special person to gain trusted advisor status with the entrepreneur. Such a person not only has to "measure up" in terms of technical and leadership knowledge, but also has to deal with some interesting personality quirks and relationships. No wonder so many outside hires end up in front of the firing squad. So who fits the bill?

I asked this question of over 500 entrepreneurs: "Looking

back, what is the one person or skill that would have helped you accelerate your business and leadership performance?"

Here's the answer I get most often from leaders of later-stage companies: "Someone who complements my skill. They are usually good with process, which is something I know both I and my company need. A CFO."

Hmm. Interesting answer. In my experience, it's only with experience that an owner/founder/entrepreneur arrives at this conclusion. The first hires are usually friends, family members, or people who exhibit much the same traits and tendencies as the entrepreneur. And in the beginning, that's just fine because the organization needs to feel like family and be flexible enough to bob and weave with the changing environment. However, once the company reaches the Engineer or Conqueror stage, it needs to be driven toward improved predictability. And that means process and measurement – which are exactly what a good CFO will bring to the party.

When I pose my question to entrepreneurs heading toward these later-growth stages, I most often get an answer related to sales: "I need a great Business Development person. That'll solve things." Makes sense, because these companies are focused on the top line. Revenue growth.

That may or not be the right answer, as business owner Duncan McGregor confessed when thinking about his early days in the printing business.

"Looking back, I remember that, when I was doing $5 million of sales, I thought if I could only make it to $10 million, my problems would be solved. When I reached $10 million, I thought $15 million was going to be salvation. My big learning was this. Revenue doesn't solve anything if you haven't built the right infrastructure and process in the first place. Worse, it actually creates more problems! If I had to do it all over again, I would have hired someone to help with that. Now that I say it, hiring someone to do exactly that would have been a tough sell for me at the time. I really didn't know what I didn't know. I'm not sure that I would have gone that route even if someone had told me. So I don't know how you convince someone who's in that position to alter their course or their thinking."

Which is exactly what this book has been attempting to do.

So, possibly the most important element of breaking free of your success cage is hiring someone who doesn't duplicate but complements your skill base. Someone who will act as your rock, your conscience. Someone who will help you build the infrastructure and process most entrepreneurs love to hate.

The Right People: Where's Your Spock?

In the *Star Trek* prequel of 2009, the movie audience was introduced to James T. Kirk and Mr. Spock in their early days at the Star Fleet Academy. Far from demonstrating the strong friendship and companionship that they would develop in later years, the two start off on a decidedly frosty, adversarial foot.

Kirk, then a recruit, is attempting to take his third shot at defeating a leadership simulation test known as the Kobayashi Maru. He wins this apparently unwinnable test, created in part by Spock, by playing outside the box and reprogramming the simulation to ensure his success.

Spock, always one to play by the rules, lodges a formal complaint to have Kirk removed from the academy for cheating. Kirk takes the opposite view. He argues that the only way he could have "won" the exercise was to go outside the rules.

It's hard to imagine two more different people! Yet time will reveal that their leadership styles are actually complementary and are exactly what is necessary for success.

One of the most common errors I see with any type of business leader, be they an entrepreneur or executive, is their propensity to hire in their own image. That's not surprising. After all, what's not to like? They're hiring themselves. The candidate is immediately attractive because they speak the same language, see the problems the same way, and quite possibly share several leadership characteristics. Of course it's not long before what attracted eventually repels. The two often end up fighting for the same space as leaders, creating animosity and distrust. The more effective route in the longer term is to hire a complement.

The first step in doing this is one of introspection and self-knowledge. You have be brutally honest about where you shine, and, of course, where you don't. The right hire is the person who will have your back and fill in your leadership gaps. A trusted advisor or significant other can be a useful mirror.

The next step is to determine, in broad terms, the type of individual (leadership characteristics and skills) who would be complementary given your own characteristics and skills. The following provides several alternative roles that I've adapted from *Second in Command: The Misunderstood Role of the COO* by Nathan Bennett and Stephen A. Miles. As you read through each description, think about the individual you believe would provide the strongest complement to your leadership style and your business need.

- *The Executor*. Has their "head down" to the business, focused on the operational details necessary for today's success (vs. the role of the CEO to be "head's up" and designing the future success of the organization). Is very strong in the execution of strategies developed by the leadership team. Willingly shoulders the responsibility for delivering the results on a day-to-day, quarter-to-quarter basis

- *The Change Agent*. Is specifically sought to bring new skills to the organization and to lead a strategic imperative such as a turnaround, a major organizational change, or a planned rapid expansion

- *The Mentor.* Someone who has broad business experience and has most likely played a key leadership role. Is comfortable with being brought on board to mentor a young or inexperienced CEO (often a founder or family member of a private firm). A rapidly growing entrepreneurial venture might seek a seasoned industry vet with wisdom and a rich network

- *The Foil.* Individual brought in to address a specific gap in leadership skills or persona. Bill Gates and two of his previous COOs are examples. Jon Shirley provided a calm, self-effacing balance to Gates' brilliant and often intimidating style

- *The Partner.* A co-leader. Just as there are doubles specialists in tennis, some executives are more effective when paired with an equal with complementary skills

- *The Heir Apparent.* The position and individual is brought in to groom or test a CEO

The individuals and roles are as varied as the leadership competencies and styles of those with whom they will work. I know you've heard it before, but it bears repeating here: the most important thing you can do for you and your business is to get the right people on the bus. Get that right and change will come easily.

Who is right for you?

After you've got the right people in place comes building the right processes.

The best-laid plans are just that – plans – unless you use them to drive action. The one page plan, introduced in the previous chapter, is the world's best planning tool only if you put it to work and make it the center of your company's activity.

The first step here is to create a yearly planning and meeting calendar. A great many of the companies I deal with have lots of fly-by meetings, but few follow a disciplined process with tight agendas, clear objectives, accountability, and follow-ups. Following is a direct quote I received from one of the companies I deal with.

> You don't know what an invaluable resource you've been in building some discipline around our meetings. Prior to your help, we'd meet with the focus of the discussion usually being whatever was the issue of the day. We'd sit down, discuss what we needed to do, and then go back to our jobs. Nothing was ever written down, so although we'd agreed to do things, they were usually forgotten as soon as we got back to our desks and the crisis of the day. We really weren't planning at all. We just lurched from crisis to crisis, thinking we were pushing the peanut ahead. We couldn't have been more wrong. We were going around in circles instead of making progress to a longer-term goal.
>
> You've brought a very simple process that builds account-ability and helps us to chart a course and stay on it. We're a totally different company! We're making some real progress and it came easily once we had someone to show us the way.

Nice words, but really, it's not brain surgery. It just requires some discipline. The system follows.

1. **Complete the one page planning tool.** (See a template of this plan, on page 122, and a sample of one filled out, in Appendix 2.)

2. **Schedule monthly two-hour leadership team meetings to review business performance and project status and agree on required course corrections.** An agenda of such a meeting will look something like the following.

Leadership Team Meeting Agenda 9:30 a.m.–11:30 a.m. July 18, 201x Boardroom
Agenda
9:30–9:40 Reconnect and agenda review (Meeting Coordinator and Facilitator)
9:40–10:00 How's Business? Status Update on KPIs (Finance)
10:00–10:15 Growth Report – status update on New Business Pipeline. (Sales or BD)
10:15–10:45 Follow-ups from last meeting (Meeting Coordinator and Facilitator)
10:45–11:00 Key project review from One Page Plan (All)
11:00–11:15 Town Hall agenda development and discussion (All)
11:15–11:30 Housekeeping items
Next scheduled meetings set

3. **Create a yearly planning calendar for all major planning and reporting activity. Put the meetings in everyone's calendar.** Following is a sample of some of the core meetings you may include in your annual calendar with proposed frequency.

Annual Planning Calendar / Core Meeting Schedules
Daily
Meetings as required to inform, recommend, problem-solve, train. All formal meetings to have written agenda, objectives, attendance requirements, and post-meeting distribution of agreed upon next steps.
Weekly
One meeting per week to update key project status and short business update. 1:1 standing meetings with key reports.
Monthly
Company-wide update Financial month-end review Monthly Business Summary, Outlook, and Action Plan
Quarterly
Update and (re)planning meeting In-depth project reviews and course correction In-depth risks/offsets financial review Informal performance reviews and updates
Annually
Accounting/bank review (if appropriate) Culture survey Client survey Personnel reviews: Objectives and Development Plans Succession and personnel review Compensation and merit planning Annual planning review and goal setting

To conclude this chapter, let me reiterate that all of the foregoing knowledge, from the beginning of the book to this point, counts for naught if the plan is not used. Execution is everything!

10
Bringing It Home

Very often when I'm speaking to groups about organizational growth, I start with the Riddle of the Sphinx. The story goes like this.

According to Greek mythology, in approximately 450 B.C. there lived a Sphinx whose job it was to protect the city of Thebes. Those wishing to enter the city would be asked a riddle by the Sphinx. Those who answered the riddle correctly were allowed entry. Those who did not became the Sphinx's lunch. Not surprisingly, the tourist trade eventually dwindled to a trickle.

As the legend has it, one day King Oedipus (yes, the same king who killed his father and married his mother) came up to the gates of Thebes and was accosted by the Sphinx.

"What goes on four legs in the morning, two at mid-day, and three in the evening?" the Sphinx asked.

Oedipus thought for a while and replied, "Why, a human, of course! On all fours as an infant, two legs as an adult, and with a cane in old age!"

The Sphinx cried in anguish. The answer was correct. It charged to the top of a nearby mountain and jumped, dying on the rocks below. Oedipus had cleared the way for all future visitors to Thebes.

The riddle speaks to the periods of change we go through as

individuals. But it also speaks to the cycle of change in our companies. There are critical points in the development and growth of a company and its leadership when permanent and significant change may occur – points at which survival itself is threatened. When the response is appropriate, it leads to growth and rejuvenation. When it is inappropriate, it leads to decline – often to mortality.

We started this journey together by looking at organizational growth cycles, specifically George Ainsworth Land's S curve. The fundamental premise of this growth model and those like it is that organizations, like individuals, proceed through well-defined stages of growth and rebirth. Understanding these stages, the characteristics associated with them, and the natural transition points from one stage to another provides a road map for leadership and organizational development. Most importantly, for us as business owners and leaders, it helps to answer the key question, **"What next?"**

All organizations and their leadership undergo transformations in their design and the characteristics of their management that enable them to face new tasks and the problems created by growth. They experience very predictable challenges at each stage. At each juncture, the organization and leaders undergo a period of stress and rebirth. Understanding where your organization and its leadership stand in this journey is critical to sustaining growth. To this end, chapter 1 concluded with a questionnaire designed to help you identify your company growth stage, and chapter 2 summarized the characteristics and challenges most common to each stage.

The next portion of our journey turned our focus from the organization to us as leaders. Chapter 3 started with these words, "Building a path to where you want to take your company starts with understanding who you really are." The skills needed to transform an idea into a company are very different from those needed to drive the company forward to a business of some size and complexity. Predictability needs to be built into the organization through process and procedure. Entrepreneurs are excellent builders and visionaries. While they may manage well, their hearts belong elsewhere.

This is the essence of *The Success Cage*. The owner-founder finds himself or herself mired in the running of the business. Most of their time is spent in managing and less on the core elements of their strength. As one of my clients put it, "I'm the one who is great at looking around the corner for my company. It's just that now I realize I'm spending no time on that and all of my time running this place. And I'm really not the person who should be doing that!"

The core message? **To grow, you must let go.**

Next, we circled back to the organization to drill down on the company itself. We did this through a general discussion of the operational elements driving organizational value beyond financials, followed by a questionnaire that yielded a Business Value Score for your business. The stronger the business, regardless of its stage of development, the greater the value – whether you're looking to sell or not.

Then came a chapter that focused on making it happen. Any journey starts with some sort of road map or guide. I introduced, with more than a little hyperbole, the world's best business tool, the one page plan, which fulfills the role of a guide for your business. It's a simple, no-nonsense, pragmatic tool that outlines your company's destination, what's needed to get there, and how you'll measure your progress.

There is a "but" however. That "but" comes in the form of discipline. It doesn't matter whether the plan is one page or a hundred. If it's not used, it's useless. And making sure that the one page plan becomes the center point of the company's day-to-day work is the most important part of driving your company forward.

Let me close by wishing each of you success with the business and your new role in it. Destiny awaits those who move beyond the owner-doer model. And let me remind you that, as you extricate yourself from the direct day-to-day management of the business, you will achieve a very important goal and receive a wonderful benefit.

To pick up on what I said in the introduction of this book, the goal that you will achieve is freedom. Full freedom of choice. You will be able to see beyond the immediate business to other opportunities. You will be freed from the daily grind that has become a major part of your life as well as the feeling that you alone shoulder the responsibility for the success of the business. Lost energy and new passions will be ignited. You will rediscover relationships and purpose.

The benefit that you will receive is wealth. Because your business is restructured to allow itself to move beyond the limitations of the owner-doer, it commands a much higher value. This value is light years ahead of the value of a business managed by an owner-doer.

Talk about a win-win! Personal freedom and a much higher return! An attractive outcome to say the least!

Godspeed!

Acknowledgments

I must admit that I approached writing this book with some trepidation, this being my second (and likely my last – of this type, anyway). For those of you who haven't been through the process, let me say it is quite humbling. It takes a lot more effort than any author would care to admit. There's always a better way to say something. There are stories that you've forgotten to mention or those that, in hindsight, would have illustrated a point better. Spelling mistakes crop up in the most unlikely of places even after several edits. All that said, for me it has been worth the bother just to be able to work with the type of people who agreed to help me.

With appropriate apologies to those I might miss, I'd like to single out several for special mention. My first thank you goes to an organization of terrific people I've had the opportunity to work with for the past five years or so. The Executive Committee, or TEC, gave me the opportunity to live and learn from some terrific business owners across Canada and the United States. Much of the knowledge between the covers of this book was gleaned from the TEC members themselves as well as the cadre of seasoned business coaches who represent the Chairs of the organization. Lynn Tanner and Catherine Osler provided their time, counsel, and experience both in supporting my first book, *Fog Lights: Piercing the Fog of Everyday Business*, and providing fodder for this one.

Tracy Dale also deserves special recognition, which I was unable to give her in the acknowledgments of that first book.

I'd like to give special mention to two individuals in the TEC family, Ian Bell and Peter Buchanan. Ian and I go back a lot farther than I'd like to admit. We were counselors at camp together at the tender age of sixteen and have great stories of friendship in the many years that have followed. Whether discussing how to help one of our fellow TEC members deal with a thorny business issue or instructing me in how to keep a putt on course across a particularly gnarly golf green, Ian has always provided valued perspective. (Not always right, mind you ... but always a strong point of view.) We've had some fun along the way, and I hope we continue to do so. Peter, as Regional Chair of TEC, provided deep perspective on the owner-operator, born from his many years as mentor and coach to this group. I tip my hat to both of you.

I would be remiss if I didn't acknowledge the members of TEC 364, my former group. In alphabetical order, they are: Cristina Austin, Paula Bass, Dianne Carmichael, Matthew Diamond, John Ferreira, Saqib Hassan, Marc Inkol, Jim Kabrajee, JP Lacroix, James Lowe, Bill McLean, Cailey Stollery, and Tony Vita. You have contributed in no small way to my growth as a coach and facilitator. I appreciate your continuing friendship and counsel.

There were many times during the process of writing this book that I needed to bounce ideas and theories off others. I counted on a very special group of individuals to provide in-depth knowledge of the entrepreneur and family business member. I owe a deep debt of gratitude to several people who dropped everything they were doing to listen to my latest thoughts on businesses and those who run them. Specifically: Kathryn Fitzwilliam, who gave me feedback on the flow of the book. Stuart Morley, who spent many an hour discussing my latest theory du jour. Michael Hepworth, who has never strayed far from his own entrepreneurial roots. Michael and I don't spend the time together we once did a couple of years ago, but he is on fast dial for me when it comes to cutting through to the heart of an issue. In this, he's a savant! Duncan McGregor, Peter Tonisson, Peter Henry, Yong Quek, Dean Kriekle, and Peter Gallop, friends and golf companions who spent time discussing business problems and privately owned companies when they just wanted to hit the damn ball! Charles Chang and Anthony Rosenfeld of Sequel Naturals, who provided keen insight into the mind and heart of the entrepreneur.

Another important contributor was Robert Gold, partner of Bennett Gold Chartered Accountants and the lead host of BusinessCast, a podcast in service of the entrepreneur. Robert was a go-to resource. Many times his deep experience as both CA and entrepreneurial talk-show host substantiated my research. In addition to Robert, I should also mention the support I received through the CEOs and entrepreneurs who count themselves part of the group I host, which meets monthly to share challenges and opportunities: Gina Conte, Devon Cranson, Marianne Gobeil, Darren Hatherell, Tony Vita. All of you have done your best to keep me grounded and on track.

On the writing side, I have been blessed to have worked alongside Rob Tait since my former days at Kraft Canada. During that time, now a distant memory, Rob and I worked as "creative" and client, respectively, on several advertising campaigns. It's not often that business "friends" attain that status outside work. Both Rob and Daryl Aitken, my former account director, have been great friends these many years following our more formal working relationship. Rob, in particular, has helped on the writing side. He is tremendously gifted, having come up with the title of this book when I had hit a wall. He has also provided me with "second sight" editorial services. My sincere thanks to both of you. Thanks also to Don Bastian of BPS Books. Don was a late entrant to the process but has proven to be an invaluable resource in the final editing and production of the book.

Thanks also to my dog-walking partner, Anne, and her husband and entrepreneur extraordinaire, David MacPhee. Most of the credit should be directed to Anne, who endured hour upon hour of early morning discussion of entrepreneurial challenges, theories, and stories. She trudged on in snow or sleet, rain or shine, listening and responding to this story and that, many times before she'd had her morning coffee. My apologies, Anne. Now that this is finished, we'll move on to other subjects, hopefully with our favorite hound Felix in tow for another couple of years at least.

▲ ▲ ▲

Finally, family.

It's somewhat trite for an author to say at this point that he couldn't have completed a project like this without the love and support of family. But it's true of this one. My wife, Peg, is a saint. (Of course, I think I'm one, too.) She listens with sometimes-feigned interest as I get up on whatever soapbox happens to be near at the time. (Sometimes she doesn't fake it at all and just rolls her eyes.) Thanks for taking the time to listen and provide input when asked. Kelly and Stacey, my daughters, are in much the same camp. Together they play tag-team in making sure Dad is getting the attention he needs, in the right dose and at the right time.

Thanks also to you, my readers, for dedicating your time to exploring the pages of this book. I hope *The Success Cage* adds something of value to your toolkit and to your respective businesses.

Appendices

Appendix 1
Characteristics, Activities, and Land Mines by Growth Stage

Architect Growth Phase CHARACTERISTICS

Entire organization created from outside-in to fulfill customer need(s)

Leadership entrepreneurial and usually autocratic

Established through vision and creativity of one person or small group of people

Direct and informal communication the norm between employees

Employees know one another

Founder speaks language of employees and customers

Founder's leadership style permeates entire organization. Vestiges of style remain long after this stage is completed – to some degree is DNA of organization

Founder hires in his/her own image. Initial organization composed of friends and family

No formalized rules, regulations, obligations, or policies and procedures

Knowledge is intuitive

Organization built around employees. Employees self-select jobs and gravitate to their strengths

No formalized HR. Employees work to joint/group problem-solve

Company works from outside-in – customers and customer orders dealt with individually

No formalized planning or infrastructure to deliver product or services

All customers known and limited in number

Organizational structure rudimentary

Founders usually entrepreneurial

Communication inside company and with customers and suppliers frequent

Employees wear many hats

Overall, a spirit of adventure and high degree of passion. Calling shared by most employees driven often by founder. Almost religious sense of purpose

Long hours, low pay. Sense of tremendous future benefit (accomplishment and monetary)

Customers drive activity

Sense of family

Knowledge is intuitive. No systems to gather new knowledge or understanding

Relationships critical, internally and between company and outside world

Control based on customer and annual P&L

Cash poor. Living on edge and from order to order

Focus is on financial viability and verification of business concept and customer value

Architect Growth Stage ACTIVITIES

Determine/gain feedback from potential customer base

Research market characteristics

Determine primary/secondary competitors and determine their strengths/ weaknesses

Use network to vet idea and go-to-market components

Build informal advisory group and use it

Define/refine primary target customer

Determine core elements of offering: pricing, manufacturing options, distribution channels and/or partners, sales methods, product offering

Fine-tune product and company point of differentiation

Create "elevator speech" in English your mother would understand

Complete five-year financial plan (using solid financial expertise), with as much solid data as possible

Build business presentation outlining compelling idea and "proof" that idea will work

Beta the financial plan through outside experts

Create trusted business advisory group with experience in start-ups and industry-specific knowledge

Create cash flow plan and review it weekly

Determine cash flow needs. Bootstrap if at all possible. Determine absolute funding needs and research debt options, e.g., family and friends, angel, VC, private equity, bank

Determine legal/regulatory requirements

Get shareholder or partner agreement in place

Architect Growth Stage LAND MINES

Idea flawed, prematurely introduced or refined

Endless product tinkering, perfectionism

Lack of knowledge of market and competition

Price discounting to drive sales

Selling equity to VC or private equity firms that don't share the vision and ask for returns earlier than business can provide

Poor financial planning or complete lack of planning

Hiring MBAs

Inexperience dampens commitment of founders

Unable to fund, undercapitalization, negative cash flow

Mistakes blow up liquidity

Founders lose patience

Mission creep, too many ideas chased, dilution of effort and focus

Inability to sell concept

Lack of talent and experience scares off required funding

Eyes bigger than stomach

Leadership conflicts (founder vs. founder or founder vs. market)

Competition

Engineer Growth Phase CHARACTERISTICS

Sales/product-driven, manufacturing focus

Beginnings of functional organization structure

Establishment of distinctive competencies and market differentiation

Primary goal generating enough revenue to continue to expand and fund growth

Managers other than founder added, power struggles emerge

Information processing becomes more sophisticated

Increasing need to centralize and build centers of expertise and functions

Employees wearing many hats approach gives way to functional experts, e.g., HR, sales, marketing, finance

Departments and functions take shape

Formal communication increases, as does hierarchy

Number of employees increases; need for coordination and communication beyond informal increases in kind

Organization becomes more streamlined and efficient, with work processes defined and refined

Systems set up across functions, e.g., inventory control, accounting, order processing, forecasting, human resources

Engineer Growth Stage ACTIVITIES

Leader moves from dreamer to doer

Expand customer base with focus on core offering

Build customer feedback loop, gain customer feedback on product/service elements in isolation and vs. competitive offerings; listen for and act on information, making this a whole company exercise, not just one functional responsibility, e.g., sales

Build market expertise and knowledge, focus on market but keep long-range sensors up by attending knowledge sessions outside immediate industry; read voraciously

Keep focus on core offering. Avoid chasing revenue for revenue's sake

Build sales, production, and financial core first – plan, sell, make, analyze

Add expertise to advisory group as needs identified

Seek "truth sayers" and consider peer advisory group

Rent expertise before buying; don't add fixed headcount or high-cost bodies until necessary; hire requirements in recognition of business development; once product is determined, focus on getting sales first, then delivering; an order triggers everything else

Minimize investment in "nice-to-have's" – e.g., office space, manufacturing facilities. Until business is proven, pay premium in short-term to rent vs. own

Build focused, formalized plan with a detailed cash flow. Build it to use it. Use it to guide daily activity and resourcing

Access debt financing if necessary. Determine equity financing needs based on cash flow projections

Create business cash flow scenarios tied to levels of business success with required actions in advance of need

Research people costs and options to acquire low-cost talent. Consider equity for highest-potential individuals only

Refine partnership and/or share agreements

Build preliminary financial analysis and reporting systems: A/R, payables, inventory, P&L, balance sheet, key performance indicators and tracking mechanisms, accounting, development of standards, and financial analysis and reporting structure on a daily, weekly, monthly, and annual basis. For smaller businesses, off-the-shelf will probably suffice

Develop formalized communication mechanisms for employees and outside stakeholders (banks, shareholders, suppliers, customers)

Develop fast, flexible communication mechanism for real-time decision making, e.g., daily huddles

Review and refine core differentiation and purpose, get customer/supplier feedback

Build compensation plan and policies

Write job definitions and define core competencies, refine accountability

Determine profitability by customer, develop program to address customer segments

Create demand forecast system, link to supply and manufacturing

Refine manufacturing processes, streamline production, create standards

Develop appropriate manufacturing skills and capabilities, e.g., safety training, recall protocol, manufacturing analysis by product, by line

Develop and implement lead generation and referral system

Build and communicate pricing policies

Create sales training protocol and training program

Develop leadership team and decision-making protocol distinct from founder

Build memory bank or company experience library

Build process to on-board new hires

Engineer Growth Stage LAND MINES

Arrogance of founder/organization

Planning on miracles

Growth too high, system and resources can't keep up

Founder is bottleneck: inconsistent, arrogant, dictatorial, attributes little importance to structure, incompetent, preoccupied with external world, little attention to detail

Skills/required competencies do not develop in critical areas

Hiring MBAs

Employee churn, loss of expertise

Founder/leadership conflict

Firm outmaneuvered by competition

Cash and liquidity crisis

Communication breakdowns, internally and/or between company and external stakeholders

Environment changes too quickly

Increasingly unknown customer base with commensurate complexity of demand

New hires dilute company focus and passion

Environment becomes more impersonal. Founder loses touch with front-line activity

Senior leadership tries to maintain reign of control/authority

Premature processes

Conqueror Growth Stage CHARACTERISTICS

Leadership has experienced their aha moment, founder/CEO realizes role they have played (lead technical or salesperson) will not work in future

Divisional structures emerge to capture opportunity as products and services expand

Active search for new markets and customers

Profit centers emerge

Information systems decentralize and increase in complexity, functional systems emerge

Full functional systems developed and replicated across divisions

Geographic expansion

Decision-making pushed out to organization

Compensation and reward system migrates to include individual/unit vs. total company performance

Functional competencies developed and shared

Competing agendas (divisional/functional) emerge

Customer interface becomes more systemized and formal

Procedures and policies developed and applied

Conqueror Growth Stage ACTIVITIES

On-board professional management

Ownership must be divorced from management

Create fact-based systems over intuition

Opportunity-driving vs. opportunity-driven

Systems-design competence, redefinition of roles and responsibilities

Build business unit and cost center structures

Expand functional expertise and operating systems beyond sales, operations, and finance, e.g., HR, marketing, legal, research, procurement

Tighten planning and coordination functions

Access geographic and additional channel opportunities

Build innovation process and testing protocol

Create formal communication channels and employee-alignment mechanisms

Tighten work processes and commit them to paper

Formalize planning structure

Create and deploy functional systems and processes across divisions and functions

Push decision-making out to organization

Build compensation and reward system that reflects individual and company performance

Identify core competencies and human capital needs

Build expanded customer policies and procedures

Establish formal resource and priority allocation mechanisms at company and unit level

Build training and development programs at corporate and functional level

Expand customer feedback and action processes

Develop crisis management skills

Expand market and competitive analysis capability

Pursue selected JV/Acquisitions

Conqueror Growth Stage LAND MINES

Decentralization fails

Systems and control mechanisms ineffective

Leadership inexperienced/unable to assert new order

Loss of control of units

Loss of purpose and employee alignment

Communication breakdowns

Loss of core customers as focus shifts to new

Growth outpaces cash needs

Competition cuts into historical base business

Acquisition fails

Conductor Growth Stage CHARACTERISTICS

Strengthened HQ and staff functions

Strong administration support and systems

Control and power struggles begin between field and HQ

Core company purpose is diluted

Sense of urgency for growth decreases

Internal focus increases, customer focus decreases

Organizational focus is on control, alignment, and efficiency

Culture increases formality

Birth of productivity focus

Decisions increasingly fact-based and studied

Markets have been mastered

Functional/product accountability increased

Management talent systems well developed

Planning systems well identified and systemized

Focus is maintenance and defense of market position

Capital expenditure focused on cost reduction (vs. expansion/new initiatives)

Competitive myopia

Compensation and succession programs sophisticated

Issues of reduced communication and cooperation emerge

Internal power struggles begin in earnest

Management of decentralized functional, product, and geographies a focus and potential challenge

Leadership by bottom line emerging

Conductor Growth Stage ACTIVITIES

Build cross-functional/unit training and development

Continue to seek growth/establish new beachheads, test and sow seeds

Strengthen communication and priority-setting mechanisms

Increase compensation systems weighting on total company performance and top-line growth

Break down barriers to customer intimacy, focus on transparency

Build organizational and process innovations in addition to product

Actively seek external/outside-in company perspective

Build efficiency and productivity goals

Increase benchmarking. Expand scope beyond industry vertical

Build human resource diversity

Encourage and build efforts to explore ideas beyond corporate ecosystem

Create programs and projects that highlight and remove bureaucracy

Acquire new competencies with better access to growth (technology/company)

Conductor Growth Stage LAND MINES

Short-term focus at expense of longer-term growth

Leadership churn and employee burnout

Financial vs. organic growth focus

Low risk tolerance

Narrowing growth idea inventory

Process paralysis

Power struggles usurp corporate agenda

Company purpose diluted

Sense of urgency lost

New competition emerges/old improves game

Renovator Growth Phase CHARACTERISTICS

Organizational climate stale or toxic

Sense of entitlement starts to permeate leadership and functions

"Glory days" phenomenon: more focus on past success than future

Form more important than function – perception becoming more important than result

Focus becoming insular and inward, develop own ecosystem

Growth slow or declining

Cost and bottom-line imperatives

Heightened activity in search of "fixes": swinging for fence, e.g., with organizational initiatives, M&A

Increased command and control leadership as company flounders

Heightened leadership and employee churn

Dysfunctional internal climate

Cynical employee base

Excessive layering or de-layering of organization in search of cost savings

Strong, informal underground emerges

Leadership self-delusion/development of self-preservation techniques

Me vs. we orientation increasing

Cost orientation becoming death trap

Renovator Growth Stage ACTIVITIES

Creative destruction

Seek avenues of rejuvenation, e.g., JV/acquisition/products/processes

Expand search to new areas of business/competencies

Seek out process and policy bottlenecks and destroy

Decommission the aristocracy

In-source select new blood

Rebuild passion and generate excitement

Reach out to customer and supplier base to support the change

Sell off old to generate funds for future

Recapitalize

Renovator Growth Stage LAND MINES

Stale climate

Entitlement culture

Form more important than results

Aggressive cost and procurement culture

Perpetuation of corporate myths and legends

Overemphasis on past glory

Individual and function over team

Death spiral (cost cuts to fund bottom line)

Gamesmanship

Competition

Loss of liquidity/cash

Appendix 2
Sample One Page Plan

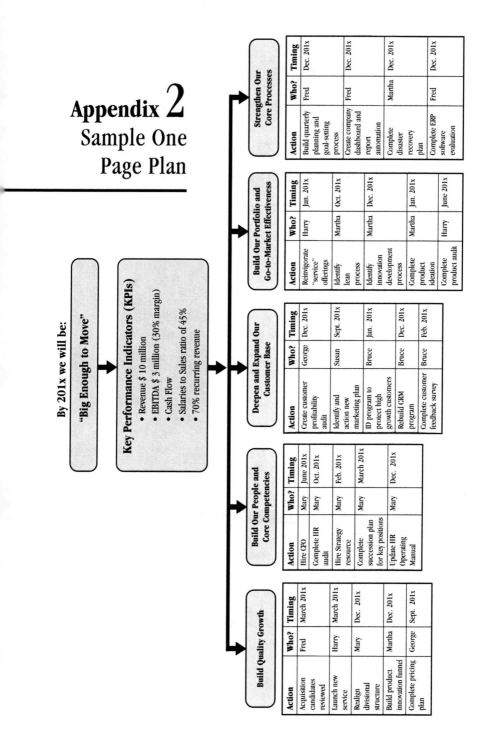

By 201x we will be:

"Big Enough to Move"

Key Performance Indicators (KPIs)
- Revenue $ 10 million
- EBITDA $ 3 million (30% margin)
- Cash Flow
- Salaries to Sales ratio of 45%
- 70% recurring revenue

Build Quality Growth

Action	Who?	Timing
Acquisition candidates reviewed	Fred	March 201x
Launch new service	Harry	March 201x
Realign divisional structure	Mary	Dec. 201x
Build product innovation funnel	Martha	Dec. 201x
Complete pricing plan	George	Sept. 201x

Build Our People and Core Competencies

Action	Who?	Timing
Hire CFO	Mary	June 201x
Complete HR audit	Mary	Oct. 201x
Hire Strategy resource	Mary	Feb. 201x
Complete succession plan for key positions	Mary	March 201x
Update HR Operating Manual	Mary	Dec. 201x

Deepen and Expand Our Customer Base

Action	Who?	Timing
Create customer profitability audit	George	Dec. 201x
Identify and action new marketing plan	Susan	Sept. 201x
ID program to protect high growth customers	Bruce	Jan. 201x
Rebuild CRM program	Bruce	Dec. 201x
Complete customer feedback survey	Bruce	Feb. 201x

Build Our Portfolio and Go-to-Market Effectiveness

Action	Who?	Timing
Reinvigorate "service" offerings	Harry	Jan. 201x
Identify lean process	Martha	Oct. 201x
Identify innovation development process	Martha	Dec. 201x
Complete product ideation	Martha	Jan. 201x
Complete product audit	Harry	June 201x

Strengthen Our Core Processes

Action	Who?	Timing
Build quarterly planning and goal-setting process	Fred	Dec. 201x
Create company dashboard and report automation	Fred	Dec. 201x
Complete disaster recovery plan	Martha	Dec. 201x
Complete ERP software evaluation	Fred	Dec. 201x

Appendix 3
Sample Business Processes and Activities by Growth Stage

Listed below are a number of business processes and activities associated with the growth of a typical business enterprise. This is not an exhaustive list. It is intended to support the development of your one page plan.

Growth

- ❏ Expand product/service offerings
- ❏ Eliminate/sell off non-strategic assets
- ❏ Acquire complementary business
- ❏ Explore strategic partnerships to access new capability/shore up existing capabilities
- ❏ Deepen penetration of existing customer base
- ❏ Build cross-sell/up-sell programming
- ❏ Expand geographic footprint
- ❏ Test alternative marketing/sales programs
- ❏ Extend core activities through outsourcing, e.g., CRM capabilities, lead generation
- ❏ Conduct cost-to-serve/profitability segmentation by product, service, and customer

- ❑ Initiate productivity program
- ❑ Complete ERP system implementation
- ❑ Complete in-depth competitive review
- ❑ Complete new product/service scan
- ❑ Execute new marketing initiative

People

- ❑ Build job specifications, role, and responsibilities for each position
- ❑ Create and communicate performance review system
- ❑ Build reward and remuneration program
- ❑ Build succession-planning system
- ❑ Identify key functional training programs, e.g., sales, safety
- ❑ Build leadership-training program
- ❑ Hire or build human resource management capability
- ❑ Build formal employee communication program
- ❑ Build employee feedback mechanism
- ❑ Complete annual HR plan (gap analysis and action plan)
- ❑ Identify and manage employee benefits plan (health, insurance, retirement, vacation, sick pay)
- ❑ Build employee on-boarding program
- ❑ Build travel and entertainment policy
- ❑ Determine union status and contracts

Customer

- ❑ Build lead-generation program
- ❑ Complete market research program
- ❑ Build understanding of customer profitability
- ❑ Build/monitor competitive understanding and activity
- ❑ Create pricing model by product/service
- ❑ Identify customer trade/credit terms and monitor
- ❑ Develop aged analysis of customer receivables

- ❏ Identify target customer segments and characteristics
- ❏ Create ongoing customer feedback program
- ❏ Identify company/product branding and creative strategy
- ❏ Build company marketing plan
- ❏ Build new product/service development pipeline
- ❏ Test marketing program components
- ❏ Build internet/social media presence and thought leadership
- ❏ Build sales training program
- ❏ Create centralized sales operations team and policies
- ❏ Identify by-customer sales teams if appropriate
- ❏ Create demand-forecasting system
- ❏ Build/acquire public relations expertise
- ❏ Identify all royalty and license agreements

Manufacturing/Product

- ❏ Build lean manufacturing process and culture
- ❏ Identify and standardize manufacturing processes
- ❏ Build product standards
- ❏ Build inventory management program
- ❏ Build procurement process
- ❏ Build quality assurance program and monitoring system
- ❏ Build risk management systems (recall, disaster recovery, safety)
- ❏ Identify approved supplier list and backup
- ❏ Create functional and cross-training system
- ❏ Build ongoing productivity program
- ❏ Build/hire logistics expertise by channel
- ❏ Create ongoing benchmarking by process/product
- ❏ Build innovation process
- ❏ Build labor-negotiations team
- ❏ Complete environmental and sustainability audit

- [ ] Build capital budgeting program and policies
- [ ] Create detailed schedule of plant expense

Core Processes

- [ ] Fine-tune accounting system
- [ ] Build billing, credit, and collections system and policies
- [ ] Create centralized purchasing system
- [ ] Build cash management and reporting system
- [ ] Identify payables program
- [ ] Create inventory control program
- [ ] Build comprehensive financial forecasting and budgeting system
- [ ] Conduct annual and quarterly business planning and goal-setting process
- [ ] Build IT infrastructure support appropriate to operations complexity. (Identify and consolidate list of hardware/software used and required)
- [ ] Build/rent legal expertise
- [ ] Complete partnership agreements
- [ ] Build JV/external development expertise
- [ ] Create corporate "memory bank" by function
- [ ] Create inventory of licenses and key contracts
- [ ] Identify transfer-pricing policies
- [ ] Assign auditors/accounting firm
- [ ] Build bank and lending programs/negotiation expertise
- [ ] Commit capitalization and ownership structure to paper
- [ ] Build real estate policies and procedures
- [ ] Identify insurance programs by business area
- [ ] Identify building codes, zoning laws, and restrictions
- [ ] Create list of intellectual property and status of patents, copyrights, and trademarks

Appendix 4
Sample Key Performance Indicators

Accounts receivable	Book-to-bill ratio (new bookings to billed-out orders (shipped))
Backlog	10-week booking average
Banking relationship	Income per employee
Cash flow	12-week rolling return on assets
Customer satisfaction	Month-end inventory
Dollars per rep	Backlog
Employee turnover	New accounts
Employee morale	New stores opened
Expenses < %	Same store sales (year to year)
Gross margins	Number of active customers
Gross profit per day	Bid list
Inventories	Number of active customers
Inventory	$ volume of quotes
Labor costs to sales	% of success on bids
New orders	Labor % of product cost
Overhead	Write downs
Payables/vendor relations	Working capital – $ and ratios
Productivity	Line of credit and line drawn
Quarterly profit	A/R over 60 days and average days
Sales to plan	New product ideas last month
Sales to prior year	Overseas orders last month
Unit sales	Overseas countries entered this year
Utilization	Working capital